KIDEX for
Threes

Practicing Competent
Child Care for Three-Year-Olds

R. Adrienne Boyd, R.N., B.S.N.

THOMSON

DELMAR LEARNING

Australia Canada Mexico Singapore Spain United Kingdom United States

THOMSON
DELMAR LEARNING

KIDEX for Threes: Practicing Competent Child Care for Three-Year-Olds
R. Adrienne Boyd, R.N., B.S.N.

Vice President, Career Education SBU:
Dawn Gerrain

Director of Editorial:
Sherry Gomoll

Senior Acquisitions Editor:
Erin O'Connor

Associate Editor:
Chris Shortt

Developmental Editor:
Patricia Osborn

Director of Production:
Wendy A. Troeger

Production Manager:
J.P. Henkel

Production Editor:
Amber Leith

Technology Project Manager:
Sandy Charette

Editorial Assistant:
Stephanie Kelly

Director of Marketing:
Wendy E. Mapstone

Channel Manager:
Kristin McNary

Cover Design:
Joseph Villanova

Composition:
Pre-Press Company, Inc.

For permission to use material from this text or product, submit a request online at
http://www.thomsonrights.com

Any additional questions about permissions can be submitted by email to thomsonrights@thomson.com

Library of Congress Cataloging-in-Publication Data

Boyd, R. Adrienne.
Kidex for threes : practicing competent child care for three-year-olds / R. Adrienne Boyd.
    p. cm.
Includes bibliographical references and index.
ISBN 10 1-4180-1273-4 (alk. paper)
ISBN 13 978-1-4180-1273-1
1. Day care centers--Administration. 2. Preschool children--Care. I. Title.
HQ778.5.B692 2006
362.71'2--dc22

2005023609

NOTICE TO THE READER

Contents

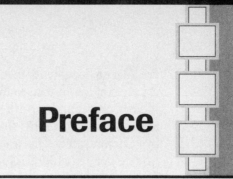

Preface

KIDEX for Threes is a proven management tool and essential resource for all child care personnel. It is one of a five-part series that includes KIDEX for infants, one-year-olds, two-year-olds, and four-year-old children. *KIDEX for Threes* provides helpful information for competent infant care in startup and existing programs. To accommodate all the demands of creating a well-planned environment while ensuring children are receiving the best possible care, time-saving suggestions are extremely important. This book offers easily accessible tools to help you arrange, plan, and organize your program. It uses a format with examples, detailed information, and suggestions to help you provide competent child care. *KIDEX for Threes* provides tools that assist communication between current and new staff members. In addition, *KIDEX* provides forms and templates for keeping active files for each child, serving as a documentation record and filing system for important information. Essentially *KIDEX for Threes* will help you, the child care professional, fulfill your role for the children whose daily care you are charged with.

HOW TO USE THIS BOOK

There are eight chapters, three appendices on perforated pages, and a CD-ROM in the back of the book. Many chapters include examples of appropriate forms and/or templates necessary for rendering infant care. The Forms/Template appendix offers blank duplicates of the examples for you to photocopy, and the CD-ROM gives you the capability to customize the forms according to your specific state standards and center requirements. The chapter examples (also indicated as figures) are there to guide you in completing your own forms when you provide child care.

KIDEX for Threes begins with suggestions on how to create a suitable environment equipped to render care and moves on to provide guidance and class management tools helpful for accomplishing physical care of the children. Where readers begin will depend on the degree of guidance they are seeking. For instance, a worker in a brand-new program would best start at the beginning and work through to the end. Someone in an already existing program, searching to strengthen only certain aspects, may choose to skip among the various chapters.

■ Chapter 1, "Snapshot of a Three-Year-Old," profiles patterns and characteristics one can expect for three-year-old children and suggestions for establishing activities of daily living suitable for the child aged 37–48 months. In this chapter ideas are introduced addressing the teacher's role for developing a multiethnic approach in the child care setting and provides means for integrating non–English-speaking children in the classroom setting.

■ Chapter 2, "Creating and Organizing a Three-Year-Olds," provides guidance for creating environments that take into account their specific needs and how to best arrange the room to accommodate a three-year-old group's natural tendencies. In today's changing world a progressive teacher must make efforts to create an atmosphere for children that clearly communicates that diversity is considered an important aspect of the learning environment. Efforts to integrate antidiscrimination guidelines with relation to age, disabilities, racial differences, cultural similarities, and class differences are necessary to foster an accepting environment for the children and families served. This chapter explores room arrangements and organization, equipment needs, how to establish learning centers and play spaces, outdoor play, selecting appropriate learning materials, choosing equipment for expanding vocabulary, choosing learning materials with cultural diversity in mind, varied learning styles, an creating an accessible environments for children with special needs.

■ Chapter 3, "Establishing an Excellent Path for Communication," provides classroom management tools to maximize communication between the children's families and all other personnel that interface with your program on a daily basis. It also provides the tools for developing written plans beginning with detailed examples and instructions for assembling a KIDEX Class Book. A KIDEX Class Book is like an operating manual for your individual group. Use the examples and templates to write an organized plan for the three-year-old group, detailed daily schedules, individual profiles pertinent to the children's specific needs, lesson plans, etc.

■ Chapter 4, "Hygiene, Cleaning, and Disinfecting," will help you establish hygienic practices such as diapering procedures, hand washing, storing personal belongings, sanitation storage, handling wet and soiled clothing for that occasional accident, procedures for cleaning and disinfecting learning materials and equipment, and promoting dental hygiene.

■ Chapter 5, "Health," provides guidance with regards to medications, measuring body temperatures, individual illness recording and establishing practices to track illness trends, and other health tips.

■ Chapter 6, "Safety," addresses accident and incident reporting, establishing practices to track accident or incident trends and how to conduct emergency evacuation drills. This chapter also provides tools for recording drills, first aid objectives instructions, and other general safety practices.

■ Chapter 7, "Facilitating Three-Year-Olds and Their Families," provides suggestions that are conducive for rendering daily three-year-old care and measures to include the family, assisting both child and family from the moment the child is received in the center to daily departure. Some examples of forms include receiving sheets, the "Introduce Us to Your Three-Year-Old" information form, individual child profiles for teachers to keep a written record of each individual three-year-old's activities and progress. Checklist templates are provided for Milestones of Development and for Activities and Play Opportunities designed for children 3 to 3½ years (37–42 months), 3½ to 4 years (43–48 months).

■ Chapter 8, "Educational Articles for Families and Staff," provides short articles of information relevant to the care and understanding of three-year-olds. Use these articles to post on the Current Event Bulletin Boards, to print program newsletters, or as a basis for parenting and/or families and staff education classes, etc. Store copies of these prepared articles and other information you collect for the KIDEX Class Book for future reference.

FEATURES

■ Over 40 forms are available to assist child care professional care for infants, including: nutrition schedules, observation sheets, diaper changing procedures, and daily medication sheets.

■ An icon identifying Best Practices appears throughout the book, highlighting the best practices.

■ The best practices identified in this book are in alignment with CDA credential requirements.

BACK-OF-THE-BOOK CD-ROM

■ Customizable forms are available on the back-of-the-book CD-ROM.

Also available on the CD:

■ State contact information is available to search for specific state rules and regulations.

■ Organizations are listed with contact information for further research.

■ Additional resources for teachers and families.

EACH STATE IS DIFFERENT

A directory listing of all state licensing agencies is available online on the National Resource Center for Child Care Health and Safety Web site at http://nrs.uchsc.edu and is referenced to you at the beginning of each chapter in the form of this icon:

To find your specific State's Licensing, Rules and Regulations go to:

http://nrc.uchsc.edu

It is extremely important for you to research the laws relevant to your own state licensing standards for compliance as well as to your specific child care center and/or facility. Although you must follow state rules and regulations, most states require minimum standards. It is debatable whether or not state requirements reflect the highest level of care also known as best practices. The term "best practices" comes from 981 standards identified by a panel of experts in the early 1990s. These standards were extracted from a compilation entitled *Caring for Our Children*, provided by three organizations: the American Academy of Pediatrics (AAP), the American Public Health Association (APHA), and the National Resource Center for Health and Safety. Best practices standards were identified as having the greatest impact on reducing frequent or severe disease, disability, and death (morbidity and mortality) in early education and child care settings. *KIDEX for Threes* incorporates these standards, and an icon highlighting best practices appears within the margins to help you identify what is to be considered best practices.

KIDEX AND THE CDA CREDENTIAL

KIDEX for Threes incorporates essential information that aligns with many of the Child Development Associate (CDA) competencies. There is a growing trend to raise standards for child care practices in the United States. Many professional organizations manage accreditation systems for early care and teaching programs such the National Association of Educating Young Children (NAEYC), National Association of Child Care Professionals (NACCP), and National Association of Childcare (NAC). Accreditation is a voluntary process designed to improve the quality of child care programs by establishing benchmarks for quality. Caregivers who desire to be recognized for demonstrating competence in the early care and education field can pursue a Child Development Associate (CDA) credential. Candidates for the CDA Credential are assessed based on the CDA Competency Standards. The guidelines for the national CDA credential through the Council for Early Childhood Recognition can be found at http://www.cdacouncil.org.

ABOUT THE AUTHOR

Adrienne Boyd, R.N., B.S.N., has dedicated most of her professional life to the early care and education field. With over 22 years experience in the field, Adrienne previously was executive director and co-owner of Somersett Heights Center for Child Care, Inc., in Indianapolis. During that time she was active in the community, serving on the Governor's Task Force for Juvenile Justice, Indiana Task Force for Step Ahead Program, the advisory board for the local high school child care vocational school, and the Child Development Training Committee Workgroup on Early Care.

Adrienne served on the National Association of Child Care Professionals (NACCP) board, as a validator for the National Accreditation Commission for Early Child Care and Education Programs (NAC), and continues to serve on the editorial advisory board for *Early Childhood News,* a national publication for child care professionals.

In 1995 Adrienne and her husband Bob launched Child Development Services, Inc. Through this venue they publish manuals, books, and child care training videos. She has received many Directors' Choice Awards for her work. She has contributed and published several articles for *Early Childhood News* and *Professional Connections,* the trade publication for National Association of Child Care Professionals.

She is a mother of two grown sons, John and Alexander, and lives with her husband in Lebanon, Indiana.

ACKNOWLEDGMENTS

Through the process of writing this material there were many individuals who supported, encouraged, and shared their expertise along the way. I wish to extend my deepest gratitude to all of you.

To my husband Bob and two sons, John and Alexander, for accompanying me on my journey as owner and director of Somersett Heights Center for Child Care, Inc.

To Annette Wilson, who so patiently transcribed my writing. To Patricia Osborn, who provided editorial assistance during the revisions of this text. And to the Thomson Delmar Learning staff who caught my vision and helped to birth this project.

To my colleagues Melissa Gaddo, Lois Struck, Tammy Moore, Courtney Callaway and Julie Butz for your supportive research, feedback, and suggestions.

To my sister Lois, who so eloquently captures the imagination of children I have had the privilege of working with throughout my early care and education profession.

To my sister Nancy for her great love of children, which is a source of inspiration to me. And finally love and appreciation to my mother, Helen Struck, my very first teacher.

REVIEWERS

We would like to thank and acknowledge the following highly respected professionals in the child care field who provided invaluable suggestions, comments, and feedback on *KIDEX for Threes* to help make it the effective tool it is.

JoAnn Brager, M.Ed.
Vice President
West River Head Start
Bismarck, ND

Cheryl Cranston, M.Ed.
Assistant Director of Early
    Education Northwest Region
    of ACSI
Hope Springs
Gresham, OR

Vicki Folds, Ed.D.
Director of Curriculum
    Development
Children of America, Inc.
Parkland, FL

Marsha Hutchinson, M.Ed., M. Divinity
Executive Director
Polly Panda Preschool
Indianapolis, IN

Nan Howkins
Administrator, Child Care
    Consultant
The Children's Corner
Ridgefield, CT

Karen Liebler
NACCP member
CEO
Children's Kastle Early Learning
    Center
Tampa, FL

Bonnie Malakie
Head Start Director
Orleans Community Action
    Committee
Albion, NY

Wendy McEarchern, M.A.,
    Early Childhood Education
Executive Director
Gulf Regional Childcare
    Management Agency
Mobile, AL

Nancy Picart, M.S.
Head Start Director
Bright Beginnings, Adventureland
    Child Care Center
Woodside, NY

Marilyn Rice, M.Ed.
Director of Curriculum and Training
Instructor
Tuckaway Child Development
Virginia Commonwealth University
Richmond, VA

Michelle Rupiper, Ph.D.
Ruth Staples CDL-UNL
Lincoln, NE

To find your specific
State's Licensing, Rules
and Regulations go to:

http://nrc.uchsc.edu

CHAPTER 1

Snapshot of a Three-Year-Old

Early care and education professionals who demonstrate thorough operating knowledge of children's normal growth and developmental traits, lay a solid foundation for a well-run program. A comprehensive understanding of three-year-old children's nature and behavior is crucial for creating an environment with realistic expectations based on their growing needs. Developmentally appropriate practices (DAPs) invite early care and teaching professionals to create and organize instructional practices that are matched appropriately to each child's developmental age, cultural orientation, social background, and individual ability. Just as we do not have control over the color of children's eyes, it doesn't work to push them to accomplish more than they can before they are ready. Understanding their natural patterns of growth and development and their cumulative social and cultural experiences helps us see what to ignore as a passing phase and what to pay closer attention to. During this next year, they need an enriched, safe, secure atmosphere, provided by patient adults who gently encourage the three-year-old's natural desire to gain independence.

RHYTHMS OF GROWTH

Around age three preschool children seem to become more relaxed and flexible than earlier. The stormy and exuberant behavior of the past six months most often calms down for a short while. The children begin to show more confidence with their newly acquired skills in all areas of their existence. Their bodies have shed the appearance of a baby and toddler, and the children begin to resemble their older peers. Their senses are heightened. Preschool children are intensely interested in the world around them and are motivated to experience it through all five senses.

The preschool child continues to grow at lightning speed. Growth seldom occurs in a smooth sequence. Much like a caterpillar that passes through a period of dormancy before emerging from the cocoon as a butterfly, a rapidly growing child often experiences calm periods, needed to practice and assimilate new skills, followed by awkward and less skillful periods vital for new growth and expanding development. Drs. Louise Bates Ames and Frances Ilg of the renowned Gesell Institute of Human Development contend that children naturally travel through periods of growth "Alternat[ing between] ages of Equilibrium and Disequilibrium . . . noting that the good, solid equilibrium of any early age seems to need to break up into disequilibrium before the child can reach a higher or more mature stage of equilibrium." These researchers' extensive observations and findings show that it is normal for children to experience greater periods of calm at the beginning of the third birth year. They experience more turmoil and upheaval in behavior as their growth accelerates, often noted in the second half of the birth year. Growth does not occur in a linear fashion: Children usually take two steps forward and one step back. On some days the young preschool child willingly shares and takes turns, and on other days reverts to more egocentric behavior, testing the limits or throwing a full-blown temper tantrum. The time spent in a "calm period" provides the necessary space to practice and assimilate newly acquired skills before nature again calls them forward.

PLAY AND SOCIAL HABITS

Around age three many children have developed a greater capacity to delay their need for immediate gratification and can wait longer. Their language skills give them some autonomy and more control over their emotions. They are beginning to understand more clearly how to alter their behavior and please others. Of course, they are novices in this area and it will take many practice sessions to "get it right." They still experience moments of that negative and oppositional behavior common during the last part of age two. This is a time they can begin to understand how their actions affect others and can learn about alternative choices. For instance, it is helpful to take the time and explain, "When you bumped the table, your brother's block tower tumbled, and he is upset. It would be kind of you to help him pick them up off the floor." Or "Perhaps you could share one of the trucks with Sam and you both can 'ride to work' together." In such situations it is more helpful to redirect and offer simple explanations rather than to give long-winded lectures. Because the children are just beginning to build social skills, many such opportunities present themselves throughout the preschool day. Gently guiding and redirecting with a simple explanation usually suffices. Learning and practicing consistent socially acceptable behavior continues to build over the next several years. Such behavior is not something a three-year-old can accomplish consistently.

As young children leave behind their toddler time, their play habits still resemble *parallel play,* where they enjoy other children's company but usually remain independently focused on their play, or *associative play,* where two or three children play near each other or are using the same equipment. Traces of self-centered behavior continue to mark their actions. Throughout the year they begin to play more "cooperatively," yet they need plenty of practice to master this more sophisticated stage of play. Young preschool children usually can only play peacefully with their peers for about 10 to 15 minutes before they lose interest.

Three-year-old children are often more interested in playing with children of the same sex and are drawn to other children who share the same interests. They continue to enjoy play-acting their life through housekeeping, grocery shopping, reading books at the library, and emulating everyday heroes such as firefighters and police officers.

Their ability to use their imagination is ignited by an enriched environment full of ideas and choices. It is not uncommon for three-year-olds to develop an imaginary friend who is quite real to them. On the flip side, their fears are much heightened at this age and they may express great fear of monsters. Of course, their personality sets the tone for the varying degrees this behavior is exhibited. Many preschoolers are afraid of the dark. A sensitive respect for their fears will help guide them through this period of uncertainty.

PHYSICAL ACTIVITY

Three-year-old children are now more coordinated and able to use their bodies with more skill. They love to ride toys—learning materials—with pedals, hop, slide, kick, gallop dance, push, pull, and climb. Not only can they tiptoe and run smoothly, but most can walk backward! Their small-muscle groups allow more refined movement, thus improving their ability to do manipulation activities such as holding a crayon with more control, using snaps and buttons on clothing, brushing their teeth, working 4- to 12 piece-puzzles, and pouring liquids from a pitcher—using both hands.

They still require supervision, because they do not have enough experience to judge the outcome of a choice. For instance, they may not understand that skating down a slide can incur a serious head injury. As three-year-olds mature, they will be able to enjoy large group activities. However, don't expect young three-year-olds to sit for longer than 10 minutes until they are around 3.5 years old, so it's important to provide an alternative activity if a child wishes to leave the group.

Because of the amount of energy young preschool children expend, it is not uncommon for them to get overtired. They are not very adept at practicing self-restraint consistently. You won't hear them say, "I need to sit and calm myself after that vigorous workout on the playground." In a busy center setting, they can easily become overstimulated by too much activity. Unless their activities are moderated, they often lose their ability to cope with sudden acts of aggression, such as biting, hitting, and scratching by a peer. A wise educator plans active sessions suitable to accommodate their attention span, such as circle games, or tricycle play followed by a period with quiet activities such as story time or exploring with play dough. The ebb and flow of such planning creates a pace beneficial to the whole group.

NUTRITION

Three-year-olds' eating habits continue to fluctuate. Sometimes parents worry because their child doesn't eat well at the center and displays a voracious appetite at the evening meal. Or has a hearty appetite at the center and pick at the evening meal. Children may eat only certain foods and refuse all others. These eating jags quite commonly disappear in time. Offer children a balanced diet, including protein, vegetables, fruits, and breads. Provide healthy snacks between the main meals of the day. Avoid snacks high in sugar content. As long as children are healthy and are not grazing endlessly on empty calories provided by "junk food," they will most naturally choose the types of foods in the proper amounts their bodies need.

NAPPING

Most three-year-olds are very good nappers. They often sleep 1½ to 2 hours after lunch. Occasionally a child shows signs of restlessness and seems tired but struggles to fall asleep. Quite often such children are comforted and able to relax if their backs are rubbed or gently patted until they drift asleep. Play soft music for the children during naptime. Music is very soothing and helps lull them into a gentle sleep.

THE GROWING LANGUAGE OF THREE-YEAR-OLDS

Preschool children's language abilities continue to evolve rapidly. Their budding vocabulary ranges from 2000 to 4000 words, assuming they are practicing in their native language. They have enough words to express their desires and pursue curiosity through liberal use of *why, how, what,* and *when* questions. They can respond to words spoken to them and can follow directions—most of the time. They more commonly use the word "I" to refer to themselves, in place of "me." Although their sentences are not always complete with full use of adverbs or pronouns, they begin to occasionally use adjectives to describe a thought, such as "I am a big girl now." It is not uncommon for them to drop words or mispronounce them. Occasionally they stutter and stumble when attempting to explain a thought. At times their minds often move more quickly than their ability to express a thought. They benefit from being with adults who allow them plenty of time and space to express their thoughts without interruptions. Gentle encouragement to use their newly developed vocabularies in conversations helps them strengthen the use of words used in proper sequence and context in the language they are learning.

It is important for providers of early care and education to recognize there is a growing population of children in the United States whose primary language is not English. Children from non–English-speaking families attend today's programs and deserve special consideration and help to bridge the communication gap. Providers of early care and education can use many approaches to meet the challenges and responding to the child's first language and customs. This subject is explored in greater detail throughout this text.

Three-year-olds continue to enjoy reading books that relate to their everyday activities. Links to faraway places, such as visiting the zoo or learning how animals live in the forest, take on a new meaning. Songs, finger plays, and stories that rhyme remain enjoyable. They particularly like Dr. Seuss books, because the stories lend themselves to this particular type of delivery. Expose them to a variety of songs, nursery rhymes, and finger plays every day. Their active imagination and enjoyment of silly humor allows them to enjoy different variations of how a story ends or to enjoy inserting their own name for the name of the character in the story. They also delight in opportunities to act out stories or simply tell the story themselves. It is a joy to watch a young preschool child "read a story to a peer." When you see that happen, you can be proud of your efforts to instill the love of reading!

REFERENCE

Ames, L. B., & Ilg, F. (1985). *Your three-year-old.* New York: Dell.

RECOMMENDED RESOURCES

Copple, C. (2003). *A world of difference.* Washington, DC: National Association for the Education of Young Children.

Davidson, J. (1996). *Emergent literacy and dramatic play in early education.* Clifton Park, NY: Thomson Delmar Learning.

Elkind, D. (1998). *Reinventing childhood.* Rosemont, NJ: Modern Learning Press.

Evans, B. (2002). *You can't come to my birthday party!* Ypsilanti, MI: High/Scope Press.

Grant, C. A., & Sleeter, C. E. (1989). *Turning on learning.* New York: Macmillan.

Healy, J. M. (1994/1987). *Your child's growing mind* (revised). New York: Dell.

Marsden, D. B., Meisels, S. J., & Stetson, C. (2000). *Winning ways to learn.* New York: Goddard Press.

SUPPLY AND EQUIPMENT RESOURCES

ECMD Early Childhood Manufacturers' Direct Supply/Equipment Catalogue. 1-800-896-9951, http://www.ecmdstore.com.

Educational Resources Catalogue. 1-877-877-2805, http://www.edresources.com.

To find your specific
State's Licensing, Rules
and Regulations go to:

http://nrc.uchsc.edu

Creating and Organizing a Three-Year-Olds' Room

CHAPTER

2

The quality of children's environment can have a significant impact on their emotional well-being. To accommodate their growth and developmental needs, healthy children need a safe physical environment in which to eat, sleep, and play. A well-thought-out room, properly equipped, clean, organized, and well maintained, will provide the environment needed to support their growing needs.

When you create the room for three-year-old care, make choices that integrate a multiethnic approach and foster an atmosphere for children that clearly communicates diversity is important. Include plenty of posters and pictures that reflect diversity, an anti-discrimination attitude and a multicultural approach. A room that fosters acceptance is one that reflects conscientious efforts to acknowledge all children's similarities and differences. Attention to details relating to age, disabilities, racial differences, cultural similarities, and class differences are necessary to foster an accepting environment for the children and families served. The type and range of diversity in a group of children will change from year to year. Deliberately seek information and clues. Careful observation of the children, their families, and the community of the care center provides clues that can help shape an appropriate atmosphere.

SQUARE-FOOTAGE CONSIDERATIONS

There is always a fine balance between meeting local government mandates and the cost of your finished square footage. The governing bodies who determine minimum suggested standards for licensure differ from state to state. Check your local governing body to determine the guidelines expected for programs in your area. Plan at least 35 square feet of indoor, usable play space per child. The more square footage available increases opportunities to create more optimum play spaces. In a room that is oversized, arrange the room to create natural boundaries. Square footage costs vary from various regions and are also an important factor to consider when determining the size most financially feasible for a program.

SUGGESTED ROOM LAYOUTS AND ARRANGEMENTS

Arrange the space to meet the developmental needs of preschool children. A well-planned space provides for their activities of daily living and facilitate safe play spaces, both self-directed and supervised. A functional layout of the room successfully accommodates large and small groups and individual activities. Large-group activities usually include the group as a whole and require adequate space for the group to comfortably assemble, for example, circle time, circle games, and napping. Small-group activities require suitable space for a smaller group of children to meet and pursue a specialized activity such as block play, dramatic play, or fine muscle activities. Individual experiences require cozy spaces that

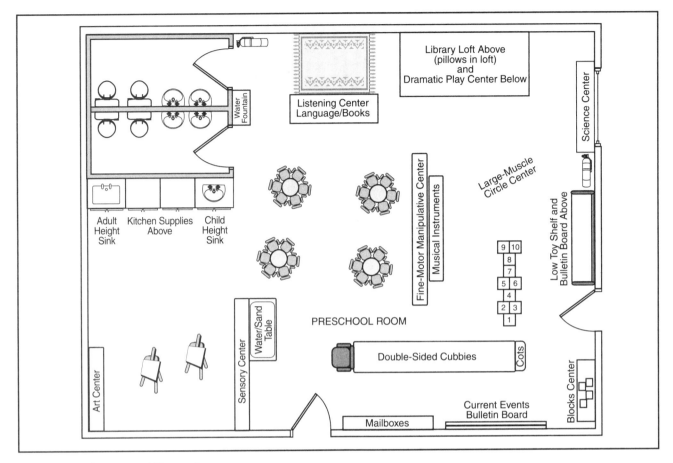

FIGURE 2–1 Suggested Room Arrangement

 provide children time alone. Create a quiet area for peaceful exploration or daydreaming without interruption from others. Mark all areas and items with labels reflecting not only English but also words that represent the diversity of the group you are caring for. For instance, if you have children from Spanish-speaking homes in the group, label in English, "bathroom," and Spanish, "baño." Although three-year-old children do not read labels, it will serve as a reminder for the staff to use both words in their conversations with the children, and exposing the children to word symbols is paramount for developing future reading skills.

 Plan to arrange the room in a manner that discourages running and sprinting about unless specifically designated for large-muscle activity. Natural boundaries can be created when learning centers and play spaces are developed. Create areas that form natural boundaries using shelving and furniture that avoid obstructing the caregivers' view. To prevent dangerous tipping if an energetic preschooler attempts a climbing expedition, it's important to secure all lateral pieces of equipment, such as cubbies and learning material shelves, securely to the floor or wall. Figure 2–1 shows an example of a suggested room with learning centers and play spaces.

ESTABLISHING LEARNING CENTERS AND PLAY SPACES

 Early care and teaching professionals create optimum environments for children by deliberately developing learning centers and play spaces. The learning center and play spaces are equipped to provide learning-enhanced activities related to each area, inviting young children to explore and play. The most common learning centers and play spaces include areas for art, manipulative activities, blocks, math, science, sensory experiences, library, language, music, and dramatic play (e.g., a housekeeping center).

Organization is an essential component for all learning centers. Provide a place for all the materials in each center. Make the containers easily accessible so the children can retrieve and return the materials in an organized fashion. For best results, use clear containers so the contents inside are easily identified. Use pictures and words to label every container used and label the shelves to indicate where the containers should be stowed. Spending time to organize the center and teach the children how to return the materials before they leave the area helps maintain an inviting learning center. The time and effort spent in the beginning allows for continuous use of the materials and equipment. Once the children understand the rules for using the learning centers, it will promote their developing sense of autonomy and require less supervision on behalf of the teacher for cleanup. A list of materials and equipment suitable for preschool children is located on Figure 2–2. Refer to that list for suggested items to stock the learning centers.

The nature of the activity level and the amount of noise the activity creates will determine how much space to devote for each learning center or play space and where to locate it in the room. For instance, in active play areas where large-muscle activities occur, devote a large amount of space. Preschool children are very physically active, and their skills flourish in an environment that offers plenty of practice in honing their growing skills. They need opportunities to pursue large-muscle activities throughout the day, which do not always require teacher interaction. Such activities may be provided for in an activity center designed for indoor usage (with proper shock-absorbing protection surrounding the equipment). A basket full of balls or "sock balls" and bean bags provided next to a basketball hoop can provide pitching and throwing practice. Place a basket or box below the hoop to catch the falling ball. The large-motor area serves many functions, such as a meeting place for circle games, obstacle courses, or circle time activities. Locate the music center in this area where the children can actively move around and create loud, joyful noise with their instruments! For best results, set up activities that complement each other in close proximity to each other. For instance, eating, art, small-muscle manipulative activities, and sensory exploration require tables or (sometimes) a source of water for cleanup. Set up these centers with floor surfaces that are easy to clean, preferably without carpet. Provide a nearby source of running water to help with water and sand activities, art exploration, snack and mealtimes, and cleanup.

The art center encourages creativity and skill practice. Preschool children are just beginning to use scissors. Choose scissors that have blunt or rounded ends to avoid dangerous poking accidents. Choose good-quality scissors that open smoothly. The children find good-quality scissors easier to handle as their skills build. Use yogurt containers to store leftover paints and small amounts of paste portioned from a larger container. Use mustard squeeze bottles to fill with paint so the children can squeeze their own. Draw a picture the size of the paint portion they should use and hang near the squeeze bottles. This will give them an idea how much to portion out. Provide a special area to hang wet paintings or heavily glued projects until they dry. Collect many types of paper and designate what is permissible to use for free art drawing, special art projects requiring construction papers, paper just for fingerpainting, and paper to practice cutting. Make available a place to store scraps of paper for future use, magazines for cutting, old greeting cards, and a wide variety of textured materials. Provide old T-shirts or smocks for the children to wear during their art explorations. Add liquid soap to tempera paint to make washing out spills on clothing easier.

Three-year-olds love to practice and mimic common activities they experience in their own lives. Create a housekeeping center with a play kitchen, beds for dolls, and accessories to

EQUIPMENT AND SUPPLIES FOR THREE-YEAR-OLDS

PERMANENT EQUIPMENT

Balance beam (6"–8" wide
    board)
Balls (6"–8")
Beanbag chairs
Bookcase
Broom
Carpet samples
CD player
Chest of drawers/costume box
Child-size sinks, stove, pots,
    pans, dishes, and utensils
Connecting blocks
Counting bears
Dishpans
Doll bed
Doll blankets
Doll carriage
Doll clothes
Doll furniture
Dollhouse
Dress-up clothes
Dustpan
Hollow blocks
Indoor climbing unit
Inner tube
Lacing cards
Large wooden pegboards and
    pegs
Large wooden threading beads
Logs
Mirror
Nesting blocks
Picture books
Pillows
Plastic hats
Play table and chairs
Play telephone
Pull-apart plastic beads
Puppets
Riding toys
Sand and water table
Shape sorting boxes
Simple puzzles
Small suitcase
Small jungle gym and slide
Small cars and planes, wheeled
    vehicles
Soft area for books (beanbag
    chairs, pillows, put soft

"things" in a wading pool, or
    a box with a cushion)
Soft toys to throw
Soft toys to hug
Stuffed animals
Unit blocks
Used food boxes
Washable, unbreakable dolls
Wooden blocks
Wooden family

MUSICAL

Blank sheet music
Clacking sticks
Cymbals
Drums 'makeshift'—metal tins, oat-
    meal containers, cans or other
    containers with plastic lids
Movement tapes and CDs to
    encourage different types of
    music
Nursery rhyme tapes and CDs
Prepared sheet music
Scraping instruments—blocks can
    be covered with sandpaper
Shakers (use film containers
    filled with rice, beans—with
    lids secured with glue)
Soothing taped music
Tamborines (make by using
    plastic lid—punch holes,
    string ribbon or shoelace with
    bells attached and double-
    knot the ribbon end)
Tape recorder
Variety of bells
Xylophones with plastic mallets

BOOKS AND PICTURES

Big books
Books on tape or CDs
Catalogues/magazines
Easy, short storybooks
Mother Goose stories
Nursery rhyme and finger play
    books
Pictures/books showing people
    in action
Pictures of many common items
    for vocabulary and matching

picture to picture and picture
    to item
Simple picture books
Touch-and-feel books

ART SUPPLIES

Baggies and plastic grocery
    bags
Butcher paper
Buttons
Cardboard
Chalk (recipe for chunky chalk
    included later)
Clay
Colored sand
Colored tape
Cookie cutters
Colorful fabric swatches
Contact paper
Cotton balls
Cotton swabs
Crayons
Dark construction paper
Dry noodles, assorted shapes
Erasers
Eyedroppers
Glitter
Glue/paste (recipe included)
Grocery sacks
Index cards
Large rolls of paper
Masking tape
Multicultural crayons and paint
    and paper (full range of skin
    colors)
Newsprint (plain)
Newspaper
Nontoxic finger paints
Nontoxic color markers
Nontoxic color chart
Packing peanuts
Paintbrushes (large and small)
Paint containers
Paper towel rolls
Paper cups
Paper plates
Pencils (big and small)
Pieces of netting material
Pipe cleaners
Powder tempera

Figure 2–2 Equipment and Supplies List

EQUIPMENT AND SUPPLIES FOR THREE-YEAR-OLDS

Sand paper
Sand (gallon container)
Scissors (blunt ends)
Shaving cream
Shelf paper
Socks (plain white)
Sponges, different shapes and sizes
Spices
Spray bottles
Stamps and stamp pads
Straws
Streamers
Stickers
Styrofoam trays (large)
Tissue paper
Toilet paper rolls
Tree leaves
Wax paper

GENERAL SUPPLIES

Balls, all sizes—include cloth, crochet, Nerf, yarn
Beach ball
Beanbags
Big tweezers
Boxes
Bristle blocks or Duplo blocks
Bubbles (recipe included)
Buckets

Camera and film
Card games (Go Fish)
Cardboard boxes
Carpet squares
Clipboards
Cloth bag or pillowcase
Coffee cans and plastic rings
Colored scarves
Egg cartons
Empty matchboxes
Felt/felt board
Flash lights
Funnels
Large marbles
Laundry basket
Lotto games
Low slide
Magnifying glasses
Matching games
Measuring cups
Measuring spoons
Metal cookie sheets
Mr. Potato Head
Muffin tin
Plastic curlers (small)
Plastic interlocking construction blocks
Plastic salt and pepper shakers
Plastic bowls and lids
Puppets
Real flowers

Sandwich bags with resealable edges
Scales for weighing objects
Several plastic jars with lids
Several matching items (mittens, socks, flowers)
Several pine cones
Several 5- to 12-piece puzzles
Several shoestrings
Sewing cards and laces
Shape cards
Shoeboxes
Shower curtain or plastic to protect painting area
Simple kitchen utensils
Silhouettes and matching tools
Small cars
Small unbreakable pitchers
Smocks
Squeeze bottles
Stacking rings
Tennis balls
Texture squares to feel
Variety of feathers
Variety of seashells
Variety of smooth and rough rocks
Windsock
Wooden clothespins with container
Zippers

FIGURE 2–2 Equipment and Supplies List *(Continued)*

play house. Equip the dramatic play area with props such as an old telephone or typewriter and dress-up clothing. Create boxes filled with props to produce a rich drama play area. In the drama area, place books that reflect different types of scenarios such as banking, grocery stores, shopping, gardening, cookbooks, etc. Change this area regularly to fuel their budding imaginations with fresh new opportunities and ideas and accommodate their interests.

The library center is one area a preschooler can experience solitary playtime. Place sturdy books, soft seating, pillows, or mats in this area away from active play. Use this opportunity to expose them to a variety of books that reflect various types of families, children from all ethnic backgrounds, and children who have disabilities. Create a quiet area for peaceful exploration or daydreaming without interruption from others. A space that provides natural boundaries such as soft cushions and pillows can provide the preschool child a place to decompress or reduce interaction for a short time period before re-entering the group.

The science area is best placed near the window for "experimenting and growing" projects. Introduce new projects on a regular basis to pique and maintain interest. Add books that explore scientific information. If the budget permits, a fish aquarium is a delightful center for observation. Pet stores often lease fish aquariums and include fish food and regular maintenance in the cost of the lease.

The block area is best situated in an area that provides plenty of space to spread out creations. Pick an area that does not get heavy foot traffic. Choose carpet that has a low pile so the surface does not interfere with the "construction projects." Stock the block area with a variety of blocks in assorted colors, textures, shapes, and sizes, both hollow and solid. Children can use them in a variety of ways such as building towers, lining them up, or using them for filling and dumping activities. Provide learning material props such as people, cars, traffic signs, boats, dinosaurs, farm animals, trees, landscaping, and books about construction. Low shelving marked with labels showing the different sizes of blocks can help the children learn to return blocks to designated areas at cleanup time.

Regularly observe to see which areas are over-or underutilized. Does the space accommodate the number of children interested in the center? Would certain centers operate more smoothly if the numbers of children were limited during its use? Establishing general rules for taking turns, sharing, and caring for the learning centers and play spaces requires more in-depth study. Many talented authors have devoted whole books to the subject. Look at the Recommended Resources at the end of the chapter for a list of books that explore the subject in detail.

Cleanup time can be facilitated by labeling all the learning materials, equipment, bookshelves, and clothing hooks with pictures that match where they are to be returned. With today's technology, digital photographs are easy to generate. Cover the labels with clear adhesive paper to protect the pictures and words. The pictures help the three-year-olds locate where to put learning materials during cleanup. Avoid using toy boxes for collecting learning materials. It is difficult for the children to find learning materials jumbled and stacked on top of each other during active play periods. Lidded toy boxes are hazardous to young children, and a falling lid can cause dangerous head injuries. Generally, three-year-old children love to be included in housework and helping. Some days they will cooperate better than others. At some moments they need encouragement and help. Learning to help is a necessary part of their growth.

CREATING AN ACCESSIBLE PLAY SPACE FOR ALL CHILDREN

McNamara and McNamara (1995) define the term mainstreaming as "placing disabled students with various intellectual, behavioral, learning, physical disabilities, and attention deficits in classes with their nondisabled peers." For the experience to be successful, a number of factors need to be considered. Evaluation of the early care and teaching staff's knowledge and experience level first must be determined to ascertain need for additional training and what level of assistance is appropriate. Assistance may include but not be limited to extra teaching aides, regular staff meetings to create and evaluate goals, guidance, or assistance from physical, occupational, and speech therapists, special education, psychiatric, and medical professionals. Special consideration may include modification of equipment, lesson plans, and the environment to include wide traffic areas that will accommodate support items such as wheelchairs and walkers.

Plan your play spaces so they are accessible to children who have special needs. Although some children with special needs need help in adapting the use of learning materials with his or her needs, most do not require specially designed learning materials to accommodate their play periods. The book *Children with Special Needs in Early Childhood Settings* (2004), by Carol Paasche, Lola Gorrill, and Bev Strom, is a wonderful resource to assist with identifying, intervening for, and including special needs children in your early care and education program.

SELECTING APPROPRIATE LEARNING MATERIALS

Learning materials are props used in play by all children. Play is valuable for all areas of growth and development. There are some basic facts to consider when choosing learning materials for children under the developmental age of three. It is their nature to explore and research with all of their senses. Choose learning materials that are sturdy and capable of withstanding repeated washing and disinfecting. Safety is an important aspect to consider when selecting learning materials and creating a safe environment. Refer to Chapter 6, "Safety," for a more detailed discussion regarding learning material safety. Provide learning materials that help develop small-muscle motor development, such as threading, sorting, buttoning, zipping, snapping, puzzles, scissors, and stringing beads, to name a few. See Figure 2–2 for suggested selections of learning materials and equipment that young children enjoy. In a group of children there will always be favorite learning materials. Three-year-old children are now capable of learning to share with others, although it is not always their first choice and they need plenty of practice. A prudent early care provider wisely provides duplicate learning materials and books to help avoid potential skirmishes.

Choosing Learning Materials with Cultural Diversity in Mind

Responsible early care and teaching programs strive to address diversity in the classroom. Special thought and planning is required to create a diverse environment that is considerate of different genders, abilities, racial, and ethnic differences encountered with our growing population. To integrate appropriate practices, choose learning materials that include all the diverse backgrounds and cultures represented in our population and among the individual children in your classroom. Make an effort to choose dolls with skins of different color, representing diverse populations. Display pictures that represent different levels of abilities, diverse nationalities, and the variety of different family structures. Seek help from the parents to explore other areas such as home foods, words the children are familiar with, music they hear in their own family environment or special holidays they celebrate. Parents will appreciate your effort to include them, in the process of integrating practices that recognize the various cultures their children represent. All parents and children should feel welcomed and see themselves reflected in the materials used.

Carol J. Fuhler, author of *Teaching Reading with Multicultural Books Kids Love,* is an excellent resource. She encourages many approaches for a teacher to integrate multcultural teachings relevant in today's diverse society. She reminds us "To make a strong connection with a book, to elicit that all important affective response, every child should see his or her face reflected in some of the illustrations. His or her culture should be explored realistically within well crafted stories" (p. 16). A teacher who continuously makes a deliberate effort to integrate and explore differences and likenesses between all people can provide an environment that communicates acceptance for all the children she or he cares for.

Vocabulary-Expanding Learning Materials and Activities

Brain development research has provided sound evidence that reading to children for as little as 15–20 minutes per day from an early age contributes to a myriad of positive brain developments. Early care and education professionals are well aware that reading helps develop children's attention span, builds vocabularies, enhances self-esteem, increases the ability to visualize and imagine, and provides many opportunities to understand words and how they create the language spoken. Therefore, provide a wide variety of books with pictures that contain simple stories, rhymes, and finger plays to encourage language development for preschool children. Selections of appropriate books that appeal to three-year-old children are listed in Chapter 7, "Facilitating Three-Year-Olds and Their Families."

Activities such as singing, playing, and listening to music support positive change in the brain and increase intelligence. Current research tells us that reading and singing to children is a simple and effective way to promote brain development. Music serves many functions in the early care and teaching environment. Dr. Gordon Shaw, cofounder and chair of the MIND Institute and author of *Keeping Mozart in Mind,* shows us how music can help us understand how the brain works and how music may enhance our thinking, reasoning, and ability to create. He contends the use of music, particularly at certain stages of development, can promote children's abilities to reach high levels of their potential. Studies have demonstrated that music such as Mozart and other classical and baroque composers strengthens the pathways in the brain for future math development. Children enjoy many different musical experiences. Expose children to a wide variety of music from various cultures, from classic lullabies to the exciting sounds of marching and parade music. A vast amount of literature on how the brain develops in the early years and suggestions for measures to facilitate growth is available. To find more information and studies related to measures that enhance optimum brain development for children, refer to the National Child Care Information Centers (NCCIC). The mission of this national clearinghouse and technical assistance center is to link parents, providers, policymakers, researchers, and the public to information on early care and education—see http://www.nccic.org.

OUTDOOR PLAY

Early care and teaching professionals are aware of the importance for children to engage in active physical play. The outdoor environment is an ideal place to encourage large motor development. Give the preschool children daily opportunities, year round, to play outdoors. Provide play equipment and materials suitable for their level of development. Playgrounds today need to offer children opportunities to use their bodies and imagination. Vogel (1997) suggests, "in the outdoor area children enjoy swinging, running, climbing, balancing, digging, pedaling, throwing, and catching" (p. 35). Think of the outdoors as an extension of your indoor learning environment. Use the time productively. Outdoor space provides a place to enjoy messy activities:

- Painting
- Chalk drawing
- Mud/sand pies
- Science activities
- Gardening
- Exploring with water (tables, sprinklers, washing items)

Outdoor time offers children many opportunities to unwind and move about. Outdoors is a place they can use their voices loudly and express movements and pent-up energy not suitable in an indoor environment. Plan a variety of activities to fuel their imaginations and break up the routine, such as

- Scavenger hunts
- Digging for treasures
- Bird watching
- Kite flying
- Hikes

- Nature walks

- Picnics

- Easy games and sports (suited for their level of development)

However, don't fill every moment with planned activities. It is important to strike a balance and provide time just for free exploration. Some children use this time to socialize and interact with their peers, and others pursue quiet activities decompressing or dreaming in a place where nature surrounds their thoughts.

Playground time requires plenty of focused supervision. Young preschool children need lots of guidance and structure to promote safety on the playground. BredeKamp and Copple (1997) remind us that a "significant amount of direct adult supervision is necessary because preschoolers' perceptual judgments are still immature" (p. 103). Avoid the temptation to cluster with other staff members for a visit. Use the unstructured time to observe and guide the children as they learn to negotiate the equipment and interact with nature.

Provide the children's families with instructions for the types of outdoor clothing they need to protect them from the elements. Let them know that the children play outdoors every day unless the elements present danger (subzero temperatures or lightning and rain storms). Weather rarely interferes with outdoor activities.

Gone are the days when a swing set, slide, and a lot of grass constitutes a playground for children. A great deal of planning is necessary to design and construct a modern playground that is equipped with safe materials and play equipment that is also accessible to children with special needs. Create a soft fall zone under and around all climbing and play equipment. A hard surface area can provide opportunities for riding learning materials. Wearing proper safety helmets when using riding learning materials is recommended to protect children from dangerous head injuries. Play equipment and surfaces need to conform to recommendations from the Americans with Disabilities Act (ADA). For guidance in building, equipping, and inspecting a playground that meets all suggested standards of accessibility and safety requirements, see the Recommended Resources at the end of this chapter.

MUSIC AND LIGHTING IN THE ROOM

Sunlight, bright lighting, peaceful music and sounds provide a sense of well-being and can encourage pleasant and cheerful feelings among those who occupy it. It is a well documented fact that children require low stress environments to thrive.

Music and lighting play a dominant role in the children's day. Music not only can be used to entertain, soothe, and educate, but it can also be used to provide natural-sounding transitions from one activity to the next. Provide several sources of music and lighting to enhance the three-year-old room and to promote a peaceful, homelike atmosphere. Soft lighting is soothing for resting and napping children. Wire the rooms to create soft lighting in the resting and quiet areas. Full-spectrum light bulbs are available in fluorescent bulbs, and provide the whole spectrum of light rays. They are a bit more expensive to purchase but will help protect staff and children against seasonal affective disorder (SAD), especially prevalent during the winter months when sunlight is reduced. For more information regarding the use of full-spectrum lighting, see the SAD Association at http://www.sada .org.uk. Skylights also provide a gentle, natural, lighting source. Table lamps are another alternative if wiring a more sophisticated lighting pattern is not feasible. For safety, secure the electrical cord to the wall. Check with your local licensing agents to determine the amount of lighting mandated during waking and sleeping times, because requirements vary from state to state.

Classroom Cleaning Schedule

For the Week of: February 4th

Classroom: Threes

	Daily Cleaning Projects	Mon	Tue	Wed	Thr	Fri	Once-A-Week Projects	Initial	Date
1.	Mop floors	C	C	C	C	C	Scrub, brush & mop in corners	CM	2/4
2.	Clean all sinks with cleanser	C	C	C	C	C	Wipe off cubbies / shelves	LS	2/5
3.	Wipe around sinks	C	C	C	C	C	Wipe/disinfect bathroom walls	LS	2/6
4.	Clean toilets with brush in & out	C	C	C	C	C	Clean & disinfect all stools	CM	2/4
5.	Clean & disinfect water fountains	C	C	C	C	C	Clean outside window door	AH	2/7
6.	Clean inside of windows and seals	C	C	C	C	C	Launder small rugs	AH	2/8
7.	Clean inside & outside glass on doors	C	C	C	C	C	Organize shelves	CM	2/5
8.	Clean & disinfect changing table	C	C	C	C	C	Move furniture to vacuum and sweep	CM	2/4
9.	Run vacuum (carpet & rugs)	C	C	C	C	C	Wipe out / inside of paper trash can	LS	2/7
10.	Dispose of trash (replace bag!)	C	C	C	C	C	Wipe underneath tables & the legs	AH	2/4
11.	Wipe outside of all cans & lids	C	C	C	C	C	Wipe chair backs and legs	LS	2/7
12.	Clean & disinfect diaper receptacles	C	C	C	C	C			
13.	Wipe off tables/chairs	C	C	C	C	C	**Immediate Project**		
14.	Wipe off & disinfect cots	C	C	C	C	C	Any surface contaminated with body fluids such as blood, stool, mucus, vomit, or urine	CM	2/6
15.	Reduce clutter! (Organize!)	C	C	C	C	C			
16.	Wipe/disinfect door handles	C	C	C	C	C	**Quarterly**		
17.	Clean and disinfect toys	C	C	C	C	C	Clean carpets		
18.									

Lead Teacher: _Ms. Marshall_

Figure 2–3 Cleaning Schedule

THE NAPPING AREA

Cots for sleeping are available in several varieties. Choose cots that can withstand regular sanitizing and store easily to save space. Pick a space large enough to create a pattern that allows adequate space between each cot. Set the cots 2–3 feet apart. Rest one child's head at the same end as the next child's feet, and so on. By laying the children's heads at different ends of the cots, you are adding an additional 2–3 feet between contact with another head. This is particularly important in the winter months, when many children have upper respiratory conditions. If the children do not have the same assigned cot every day, then disinfect the cot each day, following proper sanitation procedures (outlined in Chapter 4, "Hygiene, Cleaning, and Disinfecting").

BATHROOMS

Equip the bathrooms with flushing toilets. Special child-size flushing toilets are available so children can sit on the toilet and touch the floor with their feet. It is important to check with your licensing agency for specific guidelines on equipping three-year-olds' bathrooms, such as when they are best segregated and what the ratio of toilets and sinks are to the number of children using them. The rules tend to vary from state to state. Instruct the plumber to install at least one sink at adult height. Install a water fountain at the children's height to promote independent access and proper hydration. All sources of hot water feeding into the room require an antiscald device. Although most children are potty-trained by the time they reach preschool, occasionally a young three-year-old may still resist independent toilet use. Or a child may need diaper changing due to special needs. Examples of diaper changing and toilet training recording sheets are reviewed in Chapter 3.

STORING PERSONAL BELONGINGS / CUBBIES

Avoid spreading germs and potential cross-contamination among each child's personal articles. Personal belongings such as coats, hats, and extra clothing are best stored separately in cubbies. Consider creating a space near the entrance door or in an area that will handle heavy traffic in the busy arrival and departure hours. Commercial cubby or locker units are widely marketed in school catalogues such as Discount School Supply at http://www.DiscountSchoolSupply.com or 1-800-627-2829, or KAPLAN Early Learning Company at http://www.kaplanco.com or 1-800-334-2014.

APPEARANCE OF ROOM

It doesn't take long for a busy preschool to accumulate clutter. To keep up the center's appearance and maintain a safe environment, always work to reduce clutter in your environment and maintain cleanliness. Without a consistent effort to maintain order, the room appearance and elements of safety become compromised. A room strewn with learning materials is not only unsightly, but also creates potential tripping hazards. Young children have not mastered sophisticated coping skills. A chaotic room adds to their stress levels and can cause overwhelming feelings they do not understand. Often such an environment leads to increased aggression.

Think about the environment you create for the children in your care. Imagine every day is Grand Opening Day. Look around the room and see where a pile of clutter has begun to form. Are learning materials scattered about the room, creating a potential for tripping or falling? Are old magazines, used sipping cups, or used washcloths accumulated? A routine for handling soiled learning materials and soiled clothing are covered in detail in Chapter 4.

Child care rooms require continuous clearing off, cleaning up, and putting away. Establish regular housekeeping routines, and post a cleaning schedule for all to follow (see Figure 2–3). Your efforts to create a pleasant environment can promote everyone's level of comfort and can provide the staff with an enjoyable atmosphere to work in. It truly does make a big difference.

REFERENCES

Bredekamp, S., & Copple, C. (1997). *Developmentally appropriate practice* (rev. ed.). Washington, DC: National Association for the Education of Young Children.

Fuhler, C. J. (2000). *Teaching reading with multicultural books kids love.* Golden, CO: Fulcrum.

McNamara, B., & McNamara, F. (1995). *Keys to parenting a child with a learning disability.* Cold Springs, NY: Barron.

Paasche, C. L., Gorrill, L., & Strom, B. (2004). *Children with special needs in early childhood settings.* Clifton Park, NY: Thomson Delmar Learning.

Shaw, G. L. (2000). *Keeping Mozart in mind.* San Diego: Academic Press.

Vogel, N. (1997). *Getting started.* Ypsilanti, MI: High/Scope Press.

RECOMMENDED RESOURCES

American Society for Testing and Materials (ASTM). Retrived February 10, 2005, from http:\\www.astm.org.

Bogen, B. N., & Sobut, M. A. (1991). *Complete early childhood curriculum resource.* West Nyack, NY: Center for Applied Research in Education.

Bombeck, E. (1971). *Just wait til you have children of your own.* New York: Doubleday.

Boston University Erikson Institute. (1998–2001). *Brainworks.* Retrieved December 21, 2004, from http://zerotothree.org.

Brain Development Resources. (2002). *Healthy start.* Retrieved December 21, 2004, from U.S. Department of Education, http://www.ed.gov.

Haduch, B. (2001). *Food rules!* New York: Dutton Children's Books.

Hall, N. S. (1999). *Creative resources for the anti-bias classroom.* Clifton Park, NY: Thomson Delmar Learning.

Healy, J. M. (1994/1987). *Your child's growing mind* (rev.). New York: Dell.

Marhoefer, P., & Vadnais, L. (1988). *Caring for the developing child.* NY: Thomson Delmar Learning.

McGovern, E. M., & Muller, H. D. (1994). *They're never too young for books.* Buffalo, NY: Prometheus Books.

National website for Playground Safety (NPPS). Retrieved February 10, 2005, from http://www.playgroundsafety.org.

Schwartz, S., & Miller. (1996). *The new language of toys.* Bethesda, MD: Woodbine House.

Talaris Research Institute. *Advancing knowledge of early brain development.* Retrieved January 27, 2005, from http://www. talaris.org.

Wilkes, A. *The amazing outdoor activity book.* New York: DK Publishing.

Wilmes, D., & Wilmes, L. (1991). *Learning centers.* Elgin, IL: Building Blocks.

State Public Interest Research Groups (PIRGs)
218 D Street SE
Washington, DC 20003
1-202-546-9707
http://www.pirg.org

The Consumer Product Safety Commission (CPSC)
1-800-638-2772
http://www.cpsc.gov
info@cpsc.gov

MORE RESOURCES FOR SCHOOL SUPPLIES AND EQUIPMENT

Constructive Playthings, 13201 Arrington Road, Grandview, MO 64030-2886, 1-800-448-4115, http://www.cptoys.com.

Kaplan Early Learning Company, P.O. Box 609, Lewisville, NC 27023-0609, 1-800-334-2014, http://www.kaplanco.com.

United Art & Education, P.O. Box 9219, Fort Wayne, IN 46899, 1-800-322-3247, http://www.unitednow.com.

COMPUTER SOFTWARE IDEAS FOR THREE- AND FOUR-YEAR-OLDS

Sesame Street—Amazing Adventures

Skill Focus: story comprehension, vocabulary, word recognition and rhyming, number recognition, matching, counting, object and shape recognition and sorting, listening and sound recognition cooperation, sharing, and emotions

Blues Clues Preschool

Skill Focus: colors and shapes, spatial and size relationships, letters and early literacy, numbers and early math skills, auditory skills, and patience

Miffy Plays with Numbers

Skill Focus: Hand–eye coordination, number recognition, building vocabulary, counting and simple sums

Millie and Bailey's Preschool

Skill Focus: phonics, letters (upper- and lowercase), rhyming, written communication, understanding the elements of a story, publishing, editing, similarities and differences, quantities, size relationships, shapes, critical thinking, problem solving, creativity, imagination, listening, spatial awareness, following directions, positive communications (letter writing, thank-you cards), courtesy, confidence, and self-esteem

Jump Start Preschool

Skill Focus: uppercase letters, lowercase letters, number recognition, spatial awareness, counting, quantities, colors, phonics, prereading skills, rhymes, shapes, sizes, patterns, music, and art

Establishing an Excellent Path for Communication

To find your specific
State's Licensing, Rules
and Regulations go to:

http://nrc.uchsc.edu

To achieve an excellent path of communication between the center staff and the families they serve, a well-managed atmosphere with an attention to detail is required.

KIDEX CLASS BOOK

A KIDEX Class Book organizes, supports, and promotes classroom management and consistent care of the children. As noted in book instructions a KIDEX Class Book is similar to an operating manual for each individual group. *KIDEX for Three-Year-Olds* provides examples and templates you will need to assemble your own KIDEX Class Book for your group of three-year-olds. The templates assist the busy lead teacher and other program personnel to create, update, and maintain current written documentation with ease. They are designed for multiple uses and can be duplicated with a copy machine allowing for adaptation and branding by each individual program. Use the examples and templates to write an organized plan for the three-year-old group, detailed daily schedules, individual profiles pertinent to their specific needs, lesson plans, etc. Place the KIDEX Class Book in a visible location so when you are absent or unavailable the substitute teacher or program personnel can find it at a moment's notice. Instruct substitute teachers during the course of their training where to find the location of the KIDEX Class Book and how to use it. Emphasize with the staff and substitute the importance of maintaining a strict code of confidentiality with regard to information made available in this book. The KIDEX Class Book can also serve as a valuable reference at program meetings. It is also a good idea to share your class book with another colleague who can review your Simple Outline and Daily Schedule Outline Details to verify if the written instructions reflect your intentions.

HOW TO ASSEMBLE A KIDEX CLASS BOOK

Figure 3–1 provides a flowchart for creating the KIDEX Class Book. Purchase a 1- to 2-inch binder, preferably one that has a clear view front and an index to create about 16 to 17 sections in the book. Organize your KIDEX Class Book with the sections indicated on the flowchart. Feel free to customize and add categories to the KIDEX Class Book that comply with your organizational regulations and goals. Begin customizing and assembling sections in your book by choosing categories listed on the flowsheet. Each suggested section is marked with a star or an arrow. The stars denote sections that should be represented in all KIDEX Class Books in order to create consistency from one class group to another. The arrows denote optional choices or sections. For your convenience the table numbers of forms are listed to the right of each section heading to help locate examples and blank templates needed to assemble your own KIDEX Class Book.

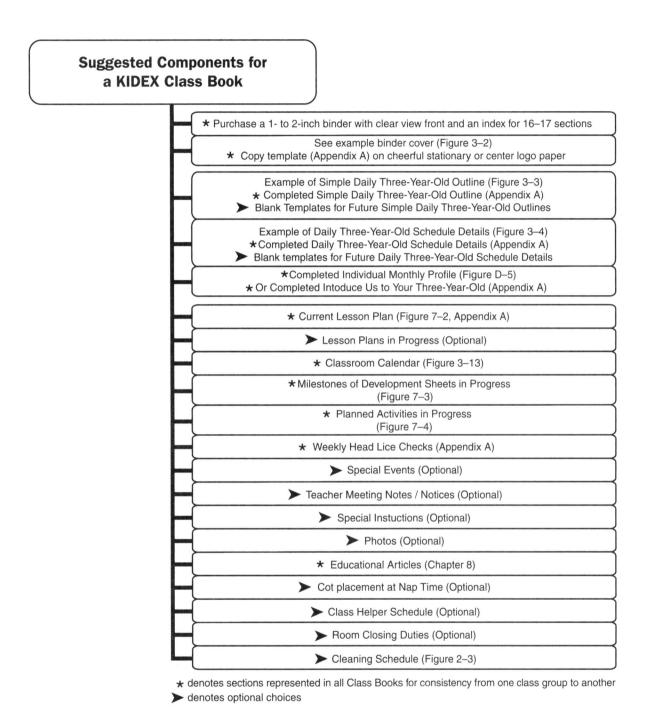

FIGURE 3–1 Suggested Components for a KIDEX Class Book

Figure 3–2 provides an example of a cover for the KIDEX Class Book. To customize a cover for your own KIDEX Class Book, use the blank template provided in Appendix A using cheerful stationary or paper with the center logo.

KIDEX *for* THREES
Class Book

The Purple Grapes

GROUP NAME

FIGURE 3–2 KIDEX Cover Example

SIMPLE OUTLINE

The Simple Outline located on page 22 (Figure 3–3) is an example of a *brief* summary of the groups' planned daily schedule. It is designed in a simple format to provide a quick orientation for a substitute teacher and for families seeking future care who are visitors at the center. The information found on the Simple Outline will give them a general idea of what is happening in the group on a daily basis. It does not contain specific details that are outlined in the Daily Schedule Details. The Daily Schedule Details is a more in-depth look at the day, providing information about where to find things, why we do this, and who has specific instructions for care. Blank templates for creating your own Simple Outline and to create the Daily Schedule Details found in Chapter 7, "Facilitating Three-Year-Olds and Their Families" are located in the Forms and Templates Appendix. This schedule provides a method for the substitute teachers and other program personnel to quickly orient themselves to your group before diving immediately into the details. Post a copy of the Simple Outline on the Current Events Bulletin Board for the parents to view and in your centrally located KIDEX Class Book for the substitute to view.

Every provider of early care and education knows children thrive with a steady routine. Try to recreate your daily routines in this written form. A successful plan will assure a consistent day for the three-year-olds in your absence.

DAILY SCHEDULE DETAILS

The Daily Schedule Details serves as a guideline. Use it to reflect the variety of many maneuvers and interactions necessary to provide for the children's diverse needs as the day unfolds. Initially the schedule may seem overwhelmingly busy, and one might wonder how a teacher can accomplish all the outlined tasks. Yet the best programs include at least two skilled adults working together. The recommended ratio for three- to five-year-old children is 1 adult for every 10 children (Kostelnik, Soderman, & Whiren, 1993). The National Association for the Education of Young Children (NAEYC) offers recommendations and guidelines for staffing ratios on their Web site, at http://www.naeyc.org.

Observe the Daily Schedule Details examples (Figure 3–4) to gain insight for creating your own individualized group schedule. When you are ready to create your plan, duplicate the blank template provided in the Forms and Templates Appendix and follow the instructions for completing it located in Chapter 7. Explain in detail where equipment or specific items are stored, such as art supplies and extra clothing. Paint a complete picture of every component listed on the daily schedule. Train all your program substitutes and volunteers how to access this information. Once the substitute has reviewed the Simple Outline, he or she can refer to the Daily Schedule Details and recreate a similar routine the children are familiar with, thus promoting a stable secure feeling three-year-olds need to thrive.

INTRODUCE US TO YOUR THREE-YEAR-OLD

On enrolling a three-year-old in the center program, provide the parents/guardians with an Introduce Us to Your Three-Year-Old form (example, Figure 3–5). This form provides the child's family a means for sharing written details concerning their child. It familiarizes the center staff with each child's unique and personal habits until they have an opportunity to bond. The staff uses the information during the child's first month of attendance.

DAILY THREES SCHEDULE OUTLINE

Early Morning	Prepare room / Children begin to arrive, hello, health assessment / breakfast / self-directed table toys and play activities / transition into cleanup / restroom / hand washing / KIDEX: My Body Is Wonderful - whole-group large-motor activities / transition into circle time.
Mid Morning	Circle time / transition into outdoor recess / restroom / hand washing / snacks / transition into next whole-group activies.
Late Morning	KIDEX: Exploring Our World or Creating My Way / transition into small-group learning centers / transition into next whole-group activity / KIDEX: Fun with Language Development.
Mid Day	Restrooms / hand washing / medications as needed / transition into lunch / serve lunch / setup for naps / tooth brushing / naptime story / rest time / naps begin.
Early Afternoon	Wakeup activities: books, puzzles, fine motor activities / naptime cleanup / restrooms / hand washing / grooming / snack time and cleanup.
Mid Afternoon	Outdoor recess / transition inside / restrooms / hand washing / medications as needed / transition into whole-group activities.
Late Afternoon	KIDEX: Creating My Way or KIDEX: Exploring Our World / transition into small-group learning centers / restrooms / hand washing / Gather items for home.
Early Evening	Departures begin / stories / somgs / fine-motor activities / Prepare room for tomorrow / Close room.

FIGURE 3–3 Daily Outline Example

DAILY THREES SCHEDULE DETAILS

Early Morning	Ms. Kimberly, the assistant teacher, opens the room conducts a saftey check of environment. She adjusts the lighting & soft music to create a peaceful atmosphere for early morning arrivals. She arranges tables for fine motor and play activities—see lesson plans in KIDEX Class Book. She welcomes the children as they arrive. The children are fairly self-directed as she monitors the group, greets arriving families, perform health assessments, and assists with separation. Children who need breakfast can eat immediately before activities. Be aware of the special allergy alerts posted in the KIDEX Class Book or on the Current Events Bulletin Board. Breakfast ends at 8:00 a.m. By 8:15 a.m. most of the groups have usually arrived and it is time to transition into the next activity. Ms. Kimberly turns the music off and says "Children, please begin to finish your activities, we will soon begin our exercises." She directs the children who are ready to use the restroom if needed and wash their hands. Once cleanup is finished, they join her in the large-motor area. Refer to KIDEX: My Body Is Wonderful on the lesson plan for large-motor activities. Or feel free to orchestrate some large-motor activities such as silly relay races, exercise, or dancing. Circle games are always a big hit. When you are ready to end an active activity to a calmer activity, be sure to use some transition techniques. This will facilitate change and focus their attention on the next activity. Ms. Kimberly generally picks a category to direct the children to their carpet squares for circle time activities, such as "Who is wearing navy blue, or has black shoes," etc. Note: With the younger three-year-olds it is necessary to build in more restroom breaks. Luke and Claire are still potty training and benefit from gentle reminders.
Mid Morning	I arrive, read Spread the Word and begin circle time activities allowing Ms. Kimberly a short break. After reviewing Spread the Word she sets up the snack center and disinfects the tables for later use. First I arrange the children around me. Carpet squares help them with space and direction. I always sit at their level on the floor. I find it easier to connect with the children, and it also encourages them to participate. Gregory usually is more cooperative and less distracted if he sits close to me. Good morning activities such as a song or finger play signals to the children it's time to focus and listen. Our circle time is our "class meeting". It is a great time to say hello and share insights they may have had since we last met. We briefly talk about our weekly theme and daily concept, the weather, calender, today's activities, and makes helper assignments. We are learning Spanish words. They are posted on the KIDEX Class Book or on the Current Events Bulletin Board. I introduce the word briefly at circle time and choose many opportunities throughout the day to use the word with the children so they can practice. Be aware of the groups' antsy factor. This is an early group of three-year-old children. If they do not want to sit the whole period, they are encouraged to help Ms. Kimberly or read the books on the table. They cannot be expected to sit for more than 10–15 minutes. Usually the more the children are hands-on in the process, the longer their interest will hold. (I choose children throughout circle time to assist with activities such as arrow changes on the weather chart). We usually

FIGURE 3–4 Daily Schedule Details Example

DAILY THREES SCHEDULE DETAILS

Mid Morning Continued	stop in the middle of our circle time for stretching and a few running in place activities. They love to begin slowly and run fast, fast, fast! Because we do this, our circle time activity usually lasts about 20 minutes. As circle time begins to wind down, we begin to transition for our snack activity and outdoor recess. Ms. Kimberly oversees the restroom breaks, hand washing, and I supervise the snack center. The children are learning to pour their own juice and select their snacks. The children will serve themselves with your guidance for correct portions. They must sit at the table when eating for safety. Again special allergy alerts are posted in the KIDEX Class Book or on the Current Events Bulletin Board. At the completion of circle time I begin to dismiss the children to put on their coats and line up to go outdoors for morning recess. We have our large-motor time (indoor or outdoor weather permitting). Ms. Kimberly takes the first group that is ready to go and I follow shortly with the rest of the group. We encourage our little charges to go! go! go! We encourage just as much participation in their body development as we do their little minds. Jimmy does have some limitations due to his wheelchair but he will try to fool you. Be sure to read activities he must refrain from listed on his KIDEX Individual Monthly Child Profile. We have a class motto: I know I can! I know I can! Be sure to have the children drink plenty of water. As we return indoors use cool-down exercises to transition. Some of the children will use the restroom, and all need to wash their hands.
Late Morning	The learning enrichment program continues. Ms. Kimberly supervises half of the children with the Learning Centers while I work with the other half on a planned activity from KIDEX: Exploring Our World or KIDEX: Creating My Way or KIDEX: Fun with Language Development. The children using the Learning Centers will switch this schedule in the afternoon with the group participating in KIDEX: Exploring Our World or KIDEX: Creating My Way this morning. Check the lesson plan for the corresponding KIDEX activity for the day. It varies each day or week depending on the unit of study. Interest Centers Note: Ms. Kimberly reviews any special instructions related to the weekly theme and makes assignments to the centers. We use the rotation method, 3 to 4 children per area. If you are in charge of the Learning Centers check for details in the KIDEX Class Book for rotating the group. Check the individual group list for the best pairing in the learning center or ask the children-they will tell you. Ms. Kimberly supervises the learning areas facilitating "teachable moments" and each center. Each center has a "helper". They are Emily, Claire, Devon, Terry, and Luke. Ms. Kimberly likes to keep them busy and focused first to help in managing group behavior. She rings the bell to indicate rotation change and as a 3-4-minute warning before cleanup. Transition into lunch preparation next. Lunch, restrooms, hand washing, and medications as needed. See the medication record.

FIGURE 3–4 Daily Schedule Details Example *(Continued)*

DAILY THREES SCHEDULE DETAILS

Mid Day	Fantastic, it's lunch time, an all-time favorite activity for our group. Mr. Anthony arrives, reads Spread the Word, and begins to help with lunch. I take a restroom break and when I return Ms. Kimberly takes a lunch break. We eat family style and emphasize the following: companionship, enjoyment of food, safety, manners, appreciation and thankfulness. Usually Kara and Daniel are beginning to show signs of hunger and fatigue; they just moved up from the Two-Year-Old Room and we nap at a later time than they have been accustomed to. We try to feed them first and move them to their cots as quickly as possible. For the rest of the children we play a pretend game they are kittens and puppies that need rest so they can frolic later. Note: This transition can be a little chaotic unless duties are given to each child to fulfill. For example: Kittens and puppies need their resting place arranged (cots & blankets), chew toys (baby doll or stuffed animals), storybook selection. Mr. Anthony supervises last-minute restroom breaks and dental hygiene.
Early Afternoon	Rest period is about 1–2 hours. Once the children are settled I read a story to them and then turn on soft music. We encourage the children to rest quietly and they don't have to close their eyes and sleep. They almost always fall asleep! Patting or rubbing backs softly is a favorite. The children's cots are placed in a designated spot. See nap / cot chart posted in the KIDEX Class Book. Mr. Anthony and Ms. Kimberly clean up the lunch area once the children are sleeping and I take a lunch break. On Fridays I have an extra hour for planning activities.
Mid Afternoon	I work on the daily reports to post on the Current Events Bulletin Board while Mr. Anthony and Ms. Kimberly supervise the children with naptime cleanup, restroom breaks, and hand washing with the addition of some grooming assistance leading up to snack time. Follow AM snack guidelines for PM guidelines. We say goodbye to Ms. Kimberly. After their rest period the children are ready to rock and roll, wiggle, and shake. Start slow and build up the tempo. The little ones have plenty of energy. Mr. Anthony and I move into outdoor recess (weather permitting) or indoor large-motor time, music and movement are next. If the large-motor activity takes place indoors, see KIDEX Class Book for planned large-motor activity noted on the lesson plan. Don't forget the winddown is very important for transition into PM interest centers. Encourage restroom breaks for those who need them, and everyone must wash their hands after outdoor play. Encourage drinks at the water fountain. Around 4:00 pm I give any medications ordered.
Late Afternoon	In the afternoon, the morning groups switch and Mr. Anthony supervises half of the children with the Learning Centers while I work with the other half on a planned activity from KIDEX: Exploring Our World or KIDEX: Creating My Way or KIDEX: Fun with Language Development. See morning instructions. As we wind down our activities around 5:00 we transition into cleanup. Restrooms, hand washing, and help gather items for home. We post

FIGURE 3–4 Daily Schedule Details Example (Continued)

DAILY THREES SCHEDULE DETAILS

Late Afternoon Continued	the final reports on the Current Events Bulletin Board. I set up fine-motor activities at the table for those who would like to participate. Mr. Anthony reads the children stories and sings songs. Departure will begin to occur, and it is important to coordinate the group's activities with Mr. Anthony's assistance plus greet parents. By 5:30 most of the children have departed and Mr. Anthony leaves.
Early Evening	See room-closing duties in the KIDEX Class Book and prepare the room for the next day of life, laughter, and smiles. Thank you, Good Job!!!

FIGURE 3–4 Daily Schedule Details Example (Continued)

Introduce Us to Your Three-Year-Old
(37–48 Months)

Date _____ 3/15 _____

Last Name: _(Enter Last Name)_ First Name: _____ Jamal _____ Middle: _____

Name your child is called at home: ___ Jamal _____

Siblings: Names & Ages: _____ Marlon 9, Desiree 12 _____

Favorite Play Materials: ___ trucks & cars _____

Special Interests: ___ kaleidoscopes _____

Pets: __ "Sugar" our dog _____

What opportunities does your child have to play with others the same age? _Plenty of cousins_
and next door neighbor Corey _____

Eating Patterns:

    Are there any dietary concerns? _____ loves to eat _____

    Does your child feed him/herself?   Independent __✓__ Needs Assistance _____

    Are there any food dislikes? ___ mushy things (oatmeal) _____

    Are there any food allergies? ____ Nuts (peanut butter) _____

Sleeping Patterns:

    What time is bedtime at home? ___ 8:00 pm ___ Arise at? ___ 6:30 am ___

    What time is nap time? _1:00 pm_ How long? _1 1/2 to 2 hours_

    Does your child have a special toy/blanket to nap with? _____ no _____

    How is your child prepared for rest (e.g., story time, quiet play, snack)
    ___ soft music and bedtime story _____

Eliminating Patterns:

    Toilet trained yet?   Yes ___✓___ No _____

    If not, when do you anticipate introducing toilet training? _____

    Would you like more information? _____

    In training? _____ If trained, how long? _____

    Is independent—doesn't require help. _____

    Does your child need to be reminded? _____✓_____

    If yes, at what time intervals do you suggest? _After meals_

    Does your child have certain words to indicate a need to eliminate? _"Pee" for urinating,_
    "make business" for bowel movements _____

FIGURE 3–5 Introduce Us to Your Three-Year-Old Example

Child wears:

Nap time diaper _____   Disposable training pants ____✓____

Cloth underwear _____   Plastic pants over cloth underwear _____

Stress/Coping Patterns:

Does your child have any fears: ___✓___ Storms _____ Separation anxiety _____

Dark ___✓___   Animals _____   Stranger anxiety _____

Being alone _____   Other _____

How do you soothe him or her?_____

Personality Traits: shy/reserved (outgoing/curious)   sensitive/frightens easily
(Circle all that apply)   very verbal (active)   restless
                           cuddly (demonstrative)   cautious
                           warms slowly to new people or situations

Health Patterns:

List other allergy alerts: _None known_____

List any medications, intervals, and route (mouth, ears, eyes, etc):

_Rx only if ears are treated for ear infection_____

List any health issues or special needs: _If he wakes up and cries out during nap, he may_

_have an ear infection._____

How often a day do you assist your child with brushing his or her teeth? _morning & bedtime_

Is there any other information we should know in order to help us know your child better?

Dad is out of town frequently; when he is in town, he usually will spend a whole day with

Jamal instead of preschool.

_____

_____Mrs. Cee_____
Parent / Guardian completing form

OFFICE USE ONLY
Start Date: _____ Full Time: _____ Part Time: S M T W T F S ½ a.m. p.m.
Group Assigned: a.m. _____ p.m. _____
Teacher(s): _____
Please keep an adjustment record yes _____ no _____ for _____ weeks.
Assign a cubby space: _____ Assign a diaper space: _____

FIGURE 3–5 Introduce Us to Your Three-Year-Old Example *(Continued)*

After the first month it remains very important to keep a current profile of each child in a similar manner provided by the families. After the first month a child has joined the group, transfer the pertinent data from the original document the family provided (Introduce Us to Your Three-Year-Old) to an Individual Monthly Profile discussed in the next section. Review and update their personal information on a monthly basis. It will continue to provide written documentation about that child and promote greater consistency with regards to their care.

KIDEX INDIVIDUAL MONTHLY PROFILE

The KIDEX Individual Monthly Profile (example in Figure 3–6) is one of the most important documents for providing a map of each child's individual preferences and needs. The KIDEX Individual Monthly Profile is an in-house document intended for in-house communication among the shift changes of staff. Written documentation of each child's unique habits and needs gives all staff substitute teachers and part-time staff vital information to care for the children meaningfully and safely at all times. Information such as a food allergy or that the child only wears a naptime diaper could easily be overlooked with changing personnel. The lead teacher spends the largest amount of time with each child and becomes quite familiar with their individual needs. By creating and maintaining a current copy of the KIDEX Individual Monthly Profile for each child, the lead teacher can assure that those important details are not overlooked.

Indicate any allergy alerts on the monthly profile to avoid triggering serious health conditions. This is a very important notation. For the continued safety of all children with known allergies, note the information here and on the Current Events Bulletin Board, discussed later in the chapter. Next mark the level of assistance needed with regard to *dietary patterns*. Most preschool children are independent with their eating abilities. They all require supervision in cutting the food to a manageable size. By now they are becoming quite confident in using utensils. Some children may still require some assistance, especially children with special needs. Note their ability to handle eating utensils and if they continue to require assistance. If they need additional assistance, specify these needs on the record. If they are using a spoon, fork, or cup without difficulty, then indicate they are independent. Note if they have any food dislikes. Young children have a very sensitive palate for taste and often reject newly introduced flavors, yet grow to love them later. Their food likes and dislikes may change on a regular basis.

Diaper changing and toileting habits are recorded next. Although the majority of children are potty trained by the time they reach preschool, occasionally a young three-year-old may still resist independent toilet use. Or a child might need diaper changing due to special need delays. Refer to a Toilet Training Records form (example, Figure 3–7) and a Diaper Changing Records form (example, Figure 3–8) for those particular recordkeeping purposes. If the child only wears a naptime diaper and uses the toilet during waking hours, record it here. The child who has just learned to use the toilet can be confused if the naptime diaper is not removed and replaced with underwear. Parents and guardians of the potty-training three-year-old also can become quite frustrated to find their child wearing a naptime diaper later in the evening because the afternoon shift was unaware of toileting/diaper instructions.

Record *personality traits* you have observed and those communicated by their family from initial enrollment information. Circle all that apply.

List any *health concerns* such as that a child with a leg brace might require it removed for 30 minutes in the morning and afternoon. If children do not have any health concerns, then indicate "None known." "Daily medications" only requires a no or yes. A reminder to check the current daily medications is listed on this line.

KIDEX for Threes
Individual Monthly Profile

Month: ___*April*___ Teacher: _____*Mrs. Carla*_____ Teacher: _____*Mr. David*_____

Child's Name: _____*Sabrina (Enter Last Name)*_____ Group: _____*Terrific Threes*_____

Age: ___*3*___ Birth Date: _*10/30/02*_ Allergy Alerts: _____*Sulpha Opthalmic*_____

Parents'/Guardians' Names: _____*Nancy R.*_____ Start Date: _*September xx, xxxx*_

When Eating Uses: independent _____*✓*_____ needs assistance _____

Food dislikes: _____*peas*_____

Diapers: _____ Nap Time Diaper Only: ___*✓*___ Toilet Trained: _____

Independent: _____ Needs reminding/assistance: ___*✓*___ Toilet training: _____

Special Diapering Instructions (special ointments, etc.): _____

Personality Traits: shy/reserved outgoing/curious sensitive/frightens easily
(Circle all that apply) very verbal active restless
cuddly demonstrative (cautious)
(warms slowly to new people or situations)

Health Concerns: _____*none known*_____

Daily Medications: yes _____ no ___*✓*___ (see med sheet for details)

Special Needs Instructions: _____

Stress/Coping Pattern: fears ___*✓*___ storms ____ loudness _____ strangers _____
dark _____ animals ___ separation anxiety ___*✓*___ others _____

Special Blanket/Toy: _____*Cuddles the Bear*_____ Name: ___*"Bear-Bear"*___

Average Nap Length: ___*1:00 pm to 2:30 pm*___

Special Nap Instructions: _____*Soft music, always sleeps with "Bear-Bear"*_____

Favorite Activities This Month: _____*Dinosaurs and Watering Plants*_____

Days Attending: Sun. (Mon.) Tues. (Wed.) Thurs. (Fri.) Sat. 1/2 days (Full days)

Approximate Arrival Time _*7:45 am*_ Approximate Departure Time _*5:15 pm*_

Those authorized to pick up: _____*(Grandmother) Mrs. R. Granny*_____

_____*(Aunt) Ms. K. Best*_____

Warning: If name is not listed, consult with office and obtain permission to release child. If you are not familiar with this person, always request I.D.

FIGURE 3–6 Individual Monthly Profile

TOILET TRAINING

Child's Name: _____Grace (Enter Last Name)_____
Lead Teacher: _____Mrs. Carla_____ **Date:** _____June 3_____

Time	Wet	B.M.	Dry	Refused	Seemed Confused	Comments
6:00 – 6:30						
6:30 – 7:00						
7:00 – 7:30						
7:30 – 8:00						Arrived
8:00 – 8:30	✓					
8:30 – 9:00			✓			
9:00 – 9:30			✓			
9:30 – 10:00			✓			
10:00 – 10:30	✓	✓				
10:30 – 11:00			✓			
11:00 – 11:30			✓			
11:30 – 12:00						Naptime Diaper
12:00 – 12:30						
12:30 – 1:00						
1:00 – 1:30						
1:30 – 2:00						
2:00 – 2:30						Awake
2:30 – 3:00	✓					
3:00 – 3:30				✓		
3:30 – 4:00		✓				Accident Changed Clothing
4:00 – 4:30						
4:30 – 5:00			✓			
5:00 – 5:30						Home at 5:10
5:30 – 6:00						
6:00 – 6:30						
6:30 – 7:00						
7:00 – 7:30						
7:30 – 8:00						

FIGURE 3–7 Toilet Training

Diaper Changing Schedule

Day: _Thursday_ **Date:** _November 10_

Child's Name	8:00 am–9:00 am			11:00 am–12:00 pm			After Nap			5:00 pm–6:00 pm			Bedtime			Wake up		
	BM	WET	DRY	BM	WET	DRY	BM	WET	DRY	BM	WET	DRY	BM	WET	DRY	BM	WET	DRY
1. Jacob			CM	MA	MA			CM		BS	BS							
2. Madison	CM	CM				MA	CM	CM			BS							
3. Matt		CM		MA	MA			CM			Home							
4. Olivia		CM			MA		CM	CM			BS							
5. Daniel		CM			MA				CM		BS							
6. Ashley	CM	CM		MA	MA			CM				BS						
7. Samantha			CM	MA	MA			CM		BS								
8. Christopher	CM	CM			MA			CM				BS						
9. Emma	CM	CM				MA	CM	CM		BS								
10. Ethan		CM			MA		CM	CM				BS						
11.																		
12.																		

Initial the appropriate box when diapering is completed.

FIGURE 3–8 Diaper Changing Schedule

Stress/coping patterns is the area to indicate any sensitivities or fears the child may exhibit and under what circumstances they occur. It is very common for imaginative three-year-old children to verbalize fears about monsters and darkness; others fear loud noises such as fire drill alarms or thunderstorms. Note these particular patterns in this section.

Young children thrive on routine and appreciate consistent naptime rituals. Describe all details such as "rests best with soft yellow duck" and "gentle patting." Add information about their current napping pattern, including their average length of time.

Activities the children enjoy will change periodically but are very important to the preschooler. All children have a natural attraction to play opportunities fueled by their growing imagination and curiosity. They hone their skills with repetitive play practice. Playing is their work, and they will flourish if their interests are encouraged. Indicate this information on the profile in this section.

Finish the KIDEX Individual Monthly Profile marking the days they are scheduled to attend, half days or full days, approximate arrival, and departure time. Authorized pickup is extremely crucial to document and follow. See section on authorized person cards later in this chapter for a more indepth discussion of how to facilitate authorized pickup procedures. In this section of the KIDEX Individual Monthly Profile provide a list of authorized pickup people for the referral by substitute personnel. Make it a solid policy that if the person is not listed, the administrative office must be consulted. Always check the ID of any unfamiliar person. A copy of their photo ID can be kept in the child's folder for future reference.

ENROLLMENT APPLICATION

Use the enrollment application to begin building an administrative file for each new child. Note this document is different from Introduce Us to Your Three-Year-Old. The application is generally stored in the administrative offices with permanent health records and legal documents. Items to include on an application for collecting general information are child's name, phone, address, home phone number, date of birth, gender, legal guardian; mother's name, address, home phone number, employer's name, work phone number; father's name, address, home phone number, employer's name, work phone number; emergency contact's name, relationship, address, phone numbers, home and work; names of other people residing with the child, their relationship, age (if under 21), all people authorized to pick up the child from the center, names, relationships; days child will attend, full or part time, medical emergency information and authorization, permission to leave with the child for neighborhood walks, bus ride to and from center, etc. (example, Figure 3–9). Immunizations are discussed at greater length in Chapter 5, "Health."

AUTHORIZED PERSON CARD

On the enrollment application, template "authorization cards" (in the Forms and Templates appendix) are mentioned under "persons authorized to remove the child from the center." Consider using authorization cards for those occasions when parents/guardians are unable to remove their child from the center due to some unseen circumstances. They might need to depend on a substitute such as a co-worker, neighbor, or family member not listed on the authorized list. On enrolling, provide the family with a couple of blank authorization cards. Instruct them to complete one and to call the center with verbal permission. Their instructions will include the substitute person's name and relationship to the child. When the substitute "guardian" arrives for the child, request a picture ID to verify the name matches the authorization card. Collect the card from the substitute, and return the card to parents on their next visit to the center.

PROGRAM ENROLLING APPLICATION

Child's Full Name: _____Jamae (Enter Last Name)_____ Nickname: _____Jamae, Bear_____

Date of Birth: _____10/30/08_____ Sex: _____M_____ Home Phone: _XXX-XXX-XXXX_

Address: _(Enter Street #/Apt. #)_ City: _(Enter City)_ Zip Code: _(Enter Zip Code)_

Legal Guardian: _____Nancy (Enter Last Name)_____

Mother's Name: _____Nancy (Enter Last Name)_____ Home Phone: _XXX-XXX-XXXX_

Cell Phone: _____XXX-XXX-XXXX_____ E-Mail: _____RusN@sbcglobal.net_____

Address: _(Enter Street #/Apt #)_ City: _(Enter City)_ Zip Code: _(Enter Zip Code)_

Employer: _____St. Joseph's Hospital_____ Work Phone: _XXX-XXX-XXXX_

Address: _(Enter Street #/Apt #)_ City: _(Enter City)_ Zip Code: _(Enter Zip Code)_

Father's Name: _____Harold (Enter Last Name)_____ Home Phone: _XXX-XXX-XXXX_

Cell Phone: _____XXX-XXX-XXXX_____ E-Mail: _____JacksonH@aol.com_____

Address: _(Enter Street #/Apt #)_ City: _(Enter City)_ Zip Code: _(Enter Zip Code)_

Employer: _____John Deere & Associates_____ Work Phone: _XXX-XXX-XXXX_

IN THE EVENT YOU CANNOT BE REACHED IN AN EMERGENCY, CALL:

Name: _Nina (Enter Last Name)_ Relationship: _Grandmother_ Phone: _XXX-XXX-XXXX_

Address: _(Enter Street #/Apt #)_ City: _(Enter City)_ Zip Code: _(Enter Zip Code)_

Name: _Patricia (Enter Last Name)_ Relationship: _Grandmother_ Phone: _XXX-XXX-XXXX_

Address: _(Enter Street #/Apt #)_ City: _(Enter City)_ Zip Code: _(Enter Zip Code)_

OTHER PEOPLE RESIDING WITH CHILD

Name: _Rodney (Enter Last Name)_ Relationship: _brother_ Age: _7_

Name: _Dwight (Enter Last Name)_ Relationship: _brother_ Age: _6_

Name: _Sara (Enter Last Name)_ Relationship: _sister_ Age: _3_

FIGURE 3–9 Program Enrolling Application Example

PEOPLE AUTHORIZED TO REMOVE CHILD FROM THE CENTER:

Your child will not be allowed to leave the center with anyone whose name does not appear on this application, or who does not have an "authorization card" provided by you, or unless you make other arrangements with the Center's management. Positive I.D. will be required.

Name: _____Nancy (Enter Last Name)_____   Relationship: _____Mother_____

Name: _____Harold (Enter Last Name)_____   Relationship: _____Father_____

Name: _____Nina (Enter Last Name)_____   Relationship: _____Grandmother_____

Child Will Attend: (Mon) - Tues - (Wed) - Thur - (Fri) - Sat - Sun

Child Will Be (Full Time) or Part Time

Time Child Will Be Dropped Off (Normally): _____8:00 am_____

Time Child Will Be Picked Up (Normally): _____4:30 pm_____

MEDICAL INFORMATION/AUTHORIZATION

Physician's Name: _____Dr. G._____ Phone: XXX-XXX-XXXX

Address: _____(Enter Street #/Apt #)_____ City: _(Enter City)_ Zip Code: _(Enter Zip Code)_

Dentist's Name: _____Dr. Janice_____ Phone: XXX-XXX-XXXX

Address: _____(Enter Street #/Apt #)_____ City: _(Enter City)_ Zip Code: _(Enter Zip Code)_

Allergies: _____None Known_____

I agree and give consent, that in case of accident, injury, or illness of a serious nature, my child will be given medical attention/emergency care. I understand I will be contacted immediately, or as soon as possible if I am away from the numbers listed on this form.

PERMISSION TO LEAVE PREMISES

I hereby give the School/Center _____Somersett Heights_____ permission to take my
                                            (name)
child on neighborhood walks.   YES __SM__   (INITIAL)

NO, I do not give permission at this time: _____ (INITIAL)

Parent/Guardian's Signature: _____Nancy (Enter Last Name)_____

Parent/Guardian's Signature: _____Harold (Enter Last Name)_____

Date: _____04/01/09_____

FIGURE 3–9 Program Enrolling Application Example *(Continued)*

```
┌─────────────────────────────────────────────────────────────┐
│  ┌ ─ ─ ─ ─ ─ ─ ─ ─ ─ ─ ┐   ┌ ─ ─ ─ ─ ─ ─ ─ ─ ─ ─ ─ ─ ┐     │
│  │                     │   │  Reverend James          │     │
│  │   AUTHORIZED        │   │  Name of Authorized Person │    │
│  │   PERSON            │   │  May pick up my child Joseph │  │
│  │   CARD              │   │  on my behalf.           │     │
│  │                     │   │  ⟨signature⟩      3/10/xx │     │
│  │                     │   │  Parent/Guardian Signature  Date │ │
│  └ ─ ─ ─ ─ ─ ─ ─ ─ ─ ─ ┘   └ ─ ─ ─ ─ ─ ─ ─ ─ ─ ─ ─ ─ ┘     │
└─────────────────────────────────────────────────────────────┘
```

Figure 3–10 Authorized Person Card

Threes Daily Observation Checklist

Child's name: _____Jimmy (Enter Last Name)_____ Date: _July 2nd_
Arrival: _____7:30 am_____ Departure: _____4:30 pm_____

	Breakfast	Snack	Lunch	Snack	Dinner	Evening Snack
Ate Partial (Less than half)		✓				
Ate Complete	✓		✓	✓	Home	

	Medications *	**Treatments ***
Time	8:00 am Eye drops	None
Time	12:30 pm Eye drops	None
Time	4:45 pm	Asthma Treatment
* see daily medication sheets for details		

Nap Times: _11:45 - 1:45 pm_ Diaper and Toilet Training Progress (See attached Sheet)
Yes _____ N/A _____✓_____
Comments: _Jimmy's "new" friend Luke_ Lead Teacher: _Ms. Kimberly_
Shift Time: _6:30 - 3:30_
pushed his wheelchair on the blacktop during Teacher: _Ms. Caroline_
Shift Time: _9:00 - 6:00_
morning recess. They enjoy each other's Teacher: _Ms. Julie_
Shift Time: _____
companionship. Teacher: _Mr. Anthony_
Shift Time: _11:30 - 5:00_

Figure 3–11 Daily Observation Checklist

THREE-YEAR-OLD DAILY OBSERVATION SHEETS

Early care and education professionals understand the importance of providing daily written communication describing each child's day. Accurate recording of their child's activities—eating, napping, and play activities—provides the family a clear picture of that day. There are several ways to communicate this type of documentation either individually or as a group. Some center policies require all documents with certain personal information to be treated individually rather than a group format; check your center's policy. Figure 3–11 provides a completed example of a Daily Observation Checklist. Consider reproducing the Daily Observation Checklist in the Forms and Templates appendix using two-part forms. Provide one copy for the parents or guardian at departure. File the second copy for two to three months keeping at least the past two months at all times. (Your local licensing agency may require a longer period of storage.)

OUR DAY, EATING PATTERNS, AND REST TIME PATTERN SHEETS

Some centers are mandated by licensing rules to create individual records for each child. Many centers choose to reduce paperwork by recording daily information as a class group rather than individually. If your center opts not to create Daily Observation Checklists, then other types of reports will serve your purpose. Our Days (Figure 3–12) provides information for the parents regarding the actual activities accomplished throughout the day. Although lesson plans are available, the Our Day form provides actual details and events that occur that day. Naptime often provides a quiet time to complete most of the information. Our Days, communicated in a cheerful, positive, nonjudgmental, informative, legible manner, gives the parents information they can enjoy discussing with their child. Eating Patterns (Figure 3–13) provides a space for each child's name and whether they ate a partial meal (less than half) or complete meal (more than half). The Rest Time (Figure 3–14) provides a space for each child's name and a place to record when they fell asleep and when they awoke. Simply gather the information using the suggested records, and post those on the Current Events Bulletin Board, covered in detail later in this chapter.

It is very helpful to have written observation documents whether they are individual reports or class reports. Occasionally parents express concerns. Use this material to provide helpful information or to review if a family conference is warranted. For example, they may be concerned their child's appetite seems to be fluctuating at home and want to compare how their child's appetite is at the center. A series of daily sheets can help track any unusual patterns. Information can provide helpful specifics needed to answer such questions. The director or program manager is encouraged to review all records at least monthly to look for consistent recording practices or spot areas for intervention where nutritional information is warranted.

NEW CHILD TRANSITIONING REPORT

Most children experience separation anxiety when they are first enrolled. Everything and everyone is new to them. They often exhibit confusion, fear, or lack of trust until they have had adequate time and positive experiences that help bonding to their new friends, teachers, and surroundings. Some children exhibit their fears through tears, temper tantrums, or the need for constant reassurance until their family returns. Younger children respond to having a welcome lap to sit on or cuddling a favorite stuffed animal or blanket. For the most part children usually begin to adjust to the group within a two-week period or sometimes a bit longer if they attend on a part-time basis.

Use the New Child Transition Report to provide the new family with information on a daily basis until their child has established an initial bond of trust. Discontinue its use when the child has adjusted to the new routines. An example of a New Child Transitioning Report can be found in Figure 3–15. The template to reproduce with instructions for completing is found in the Forms and Templates Appendix.

HOW TO CREATE A CURRENT EVENTS BULLETIN BOARD

In a busy preschool room time is of the essence. A Current Events Bulletin Board can provide a centrally located place to post ongoing messages. It is an important center for communications. Current Events Bulletin Board can provide a means for communication among the

OUR DAY

Group Name: _____The Purple Grapes_____

DATE _____January 5th_____ Day of Week _____Monday_____

Early morning activities/centers: (Beginning the day during morning arrival)

Set up airpot and city toys

Dramatic Play Center - Rocked our babies & fed them

Played with our new puzzles

***KIDEX Fun with Language and Telling Tales*: Activities to build our vocabulary were:**

Sang "Twinkle Twinkle Little Star"

Finger plays & songs we sang today were:

Finger play - "No more Monkeys Jumping on the Bed"

Circle Time Concept: _____Sleeping_____

Our morning outdoor activity was:

Chased "fire flies & tried to catch night fairies"

***KIDEX My Body is Wonderful*: Activities to exercise our fine and large muscles were:**

Slipper races and pillow jumps

Our morning project was:

Blanket folding

"Tuck me in"

AFTERNOON

***KIDEX Exploring My World/Creating My Way*: Our creative/sensory activities were:**

Tooth brush painting

Quilt square counting

The story we read was:

"When Cats Dream" by Dave Pilkey

Our afternoon outdoor activity was:

Took our babies and teddy bears for a walk

Swinging and sliding

Late afternoon activities/centers: (Ending the day during departures)

Listened to Good-Night Owl book on tape

Brushed and combed our hair

"ate bedtime snacks"

Extra activities today were:

Played in our pajamas

FIGURE 3–12 An Example of Documenting "Our Day"

EATING PATTERNS

Classroom: _____ Week of: _____

Child's Name	Mon Breakfast	Mon Snack	Mon Lunch	Mon Snack	Mon Dinner	Mon Snack	Tue Breakfast	Tue Snack	Tue Lunch	Tue Snack	Tue Dinner	Tue Snack	Wed Breakfast	Wed Snack	Wed Lunch	Wed Snack	Wed Dinner	Wed Snack	Thu Breakfast	Thu Snack	Thu Lunch	Thu Snack	Thu Dinner	Thu Snack	Fri Breakfast	Fri Snack	Fri Lunch	Fri Snack	Fri Dinner	Fri Snack	Sat Breakfast	Sat Snack	Sat Lunch	Sat Snack	Sat Dinner	Sat Snack	Sun Breakfast	Sun Snack	Sun Lunch	Sun Snack	Sun Dinner	Sun Snack
Erin (Enter Last Name)	C	C	P	C			P	C	C	P			C	C	C	C			P	C	C	P			C	C	P	C														
Olivia (Enter Last Name)	C	C	C	C			P	C	C	P			C	C	P	C			C	C	C	P	P	C	P	C	C	P														
Xavier (Enter Last Name)																															P	P	C	C	P	C		P	P	C	C	P
Julian (Enter Last Name)	C	C	P	C			P	C	C	P			C	P	P	C	C	P	P	P	C	P			C	C	C	C	C	P												
Sheila (Enter Last Name)													C	C	C	C									C	P	P	C											C	C	P	C
Marta (Enter Last Name)			P	C	C	C		C	C		C								C	C	C	C	P	C							C	C	C	C	C	P						
Isaiah (Enter Last Name)													C	C	C	C	C		C	C	C	P			C	C	P	C	C	C												
Justin (Enter Last Name)							P	C	C	P			C	P	P	C			P	C	C	P				P	P	C	C	P	P	P	C	P								
Olivia (Enter Last Name)								C	C	P	C	C	C	C	C	C	P		C	C	C	C	C								P	P	C	P								
Dephina (Enter Last Name)		P	C	C	P	C	C	P	C	C			C	C	C	C	P		C	C	C	C	C		C	C	P	C	P				C				C	C	P	C	P	
Jackson (Enter Last Name)							C	C	C	C			P	P	P	C	C		C	C	C	C			P	P	C	C			P	P	C	C	P							
Isaac (Enter Last Name)							P	C	C	C			C	C	C	C			P	C	P	C			P	C	C	C			C	C	C	C	C		C	C	C	C	P	
Maggie (Enter Last Name)	P	P	C	C									C		C	P									P	P	C	P					C									
Mary Beth (Enter Last Name)	C	C	P	P	C								C	C	C	C									C	P	C	C			C	C										

C = Complete
P = Ate Partial (less than half)

FIGURE 3–13 Documenting Eating Patterns

Rest Time

Classroom The Butterflies **Week of** Feb 23rd - 29th

Name	Mon Asleep	Mon Awake	Mon Reading	Tue Asleep	Tue Awake	Tue Reading	Wed Asleep	Wed Awake	Wed Reading	Thu Asleep	Thu Awake	Thu Reading	Fri Asleep	Fri Awake	Fri Reading	Sat Asleep	Sat Awake	Sat Reading	Sun Asleep	Sun Awake	Sun Reading
Sabrina (Enter Last Name)			✓	1:00 PM	1:30 PM				✓	1:00 PM	1:15 PM				✓						
Andrea (Enter Last Name)							1:30 PM	2:30 PM		1:15 PM	2:00 PM		1:00 PM	2:00 PM							
Asra (Enter Last Name)			✓			✓	1:30 PM	2:15 PM				✓	1:00 PM	2:00 PM							
Collin (Enter Last Name)	1:00 PM	2:15 PM							✓			✓	1:15 PM	2:30 PM		1:00 PM	2:00 PM		1:00 PM	2:30 PM	
Isiah (Enter Last Name)				1:15 PM	2:30 PM		1:30 PM	2:00 PM		1:15 PM	2:15 PM		1:30 PM	2:00 PM				✓			✓
David (Enter Last Name)									✓			✓	1:15 PM	2:00 PM							
Joseph (Enter Last Name)	1:00 PM	2:00 PM				✓	1:15 PM	2:15 PM		1:30 PM	2:30 PM				✓						
Migel (Enter Last Name)							1:30 PM	2:00 PM				✓			✓	2:00 PM	2:30 PM		2:15 PM	2:30 PM	
Hunter (Enter Last Name)							1:00 PM	2:00 PM				✓	1:00 PM	2:15 PM		1:15 PM	2:30 PM		1:00 PM	2:30 PM	
Cedrick (Enter Last Name)	1:15 PM	2:30 PM				✓			✓	1:30 PM	2:30 PM				✓						
Aiden (Enter Last Name)	1:00 PM	1:30 PM		1:30 PM	2:00 PM		1:15 PM	2:15 PM		1:30 PM	2:30 PM		1:15 PM	2:30 PM							
Jackson (Enter Last Name)									✓	1:00 PM	1:30 PM		1:30 PM	2:30 PM				✓			✓
Simone (Enter Last Name)	1:45 PM	2:30 PM		1:45 PM	2:15 PM		1:00 PM	2:15 PM		1:30 PM	2:00 PM		1:45 PM	2:30 PM							
Kara (Enter Last Name)	1:30 PM	2:15 PM				✓			✓	1:45 PM	2:15 PM				✓						

FIGURE 3–14 Documenting Rest Time

Child Transitioning Report

Name ___Clair (Enter Last Name)___   Teacher ___Ms. Julie___

Date of Report ___January 7___   Teacher ___Mr. Anthony___

Day 1 2 3 4 5 6 7 8 9 10 11 12 ⑬ 14 15

	NOT YET	SOME	FREQUENTLY
Played with learning materials			✓
Participated in activities		✓	
Played with the children		✓	

Appetite	COMPLETE	PARTIAL (Less than half)
Breakfast appetite		✓
AM snack appetite	✓	
Lunch appetite	✓	
PM snack appetite	✓	
Dinner appetite		

Rest Time

Indicate time   From _12:30 pm_ To _2:00 pm_

Bowel & bladder pattern (See diaper changing sheet if applicable)

Overall day

Great! ___✓___ *Seem comfortable with new environment*

Fair _____ *Adjustments to the new group and environment will improve as your child grows accustomed to the new environment*

Staff Comments: _Clair joined the group today. She enjoys sitting next to Emily at Circle_ _Time and Lunch._

Parent's Comments or Questions (If any): _Clair can't wait for pajama day_

Use for 1-3 weeks until the new child feels comfortable with the group.

FIGURE 3–15 Child Transitioning Report

program, current participating families, and future families touring your facility. It will save busy teachers from the task of repeating information to each individual family and reduces the chance information will not be disseminated to everyone. Look at Figure 3–16 for an example of the Current Events Bulletin Board.

Create a bulletin board, and decorate it with a seasonal theme. Involve the children with this project. They can plan and design the board with their ideas. It will reduce the need to change the overall board every month and will only require changing daily and monthly communication pieces. Keep a digital camera on hand to create pictures that can be printed quickly. Change the pictures often on the bulletin board to continuously attract families to this important information. Hang a bulletin board near the room entrance where everyone passes by. The following lists suggested items to post on the class Current Events Bulletin Board. Add items you feel are vital to your rooms' operation.

Current Events Bulletin Board

Schedule outline	Use this area to post the general schedule for the group
Future events	Here is a great place to post future events for example or a scheduled visit from "Charlie" the pet pig, or a celebration of the monthly birthdays.
Health news	Choose articles from Chapter 8 to explain a recent exposure to a communicable disease and types of symptoms to watch for.
Nutrition and menu information	To reduce writing duplicate information, post a copy of your menu for the day, week, or month at a time. Many families find this information helpful for planning home meals that complement the center meals. Refer to Figure 3–17 for an example of a daily menu.
Parent articles	Post information relevant to three-year-olds such as a schedule of parenting classes offered in the community.
Calendars and center newsletter	If your center creates a monthly newsletter or calendar post current copies here. Find examples of both on Figures 3–18 and 3-19.
*Allergy postings**	Post a listing indicating the child's name and known allergies. Collect this information from the KIDEX Individual Monthly Profile.
Our day	Use these to "tell" parents about the day and the activities the children completed.
*Eating patterns**	Used to describe each individual child's appetite pattern each day, that week, on a group form.
*Rest time**	Used to describe each individual child's rest time that day, for the week, on a group form.

* Check your center's policies with regards to displaying personal information such as eating and rest time patterns. Some centers find certain material too personal to share as a group and only feel comfortable with the use of individual reports.

BIRTHDAY BULLETIN BOARDS

Creating a birthday bulletin board is a wonderful way to spotlight a special quality each child possesses. Create a theme for the year and add names as children join your group. An

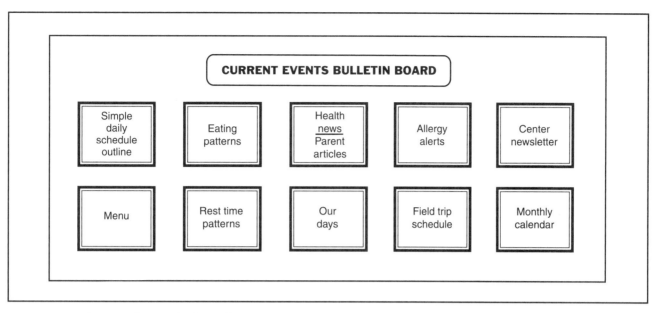

FIGURE 3–16 Current Events Bulletin Board

Our Menu Today

Date _Thursday, June 14_

Breakfast _Milk 2% (3/4 cup)_

Strawberries (1/2 cup)

Cream cheese (1 tbsp)

Bagel, cinnamon raisin (1/2 serving, 0.5 oz)

Snack _Cheese (1/2 oz)_

Apple juice 100% vitamin C (1/4 cup)

Wheat crackers (1/2 serving/0.5 oz)

Lunch _Milk 2% (1/2 cup)_

Baked chicken (1/2 oz)

Oven fries (2 pieces)

Green beans (1/4 cup) and carrots (1/4 cup)

Fruit cocktail (1/4 cup)

Snack _Blueberry low fat yogurt (2 oz)_

Graham crackers (1 square)

Water (2-4 oz)

FIGURE 3–17 Our Menu Today

Center Calendar

June

Sunday	Monday	Tuesday	Wednesday	**Thursday**	Friday	Saturday
Weekly Theme: 500 Festival				1	2	3 Deep Cleaning Day 8–4 pm
4 Weekly Theme: Fun Week	5 Hunter 5th & Andrew 4th Birthday	6 First Aid & CPR Class Staff & Parents	7 Roderick 3rd Birthday	8	9 Kelsi 4th Birthday	10
11 Weekly Theme: Family & Friends	12 Lead Teacher Meeting 6:15 pm	13	14 Summer Camp Jr's Field Trip to Bowling Alley	15 Summer Camp Sr's Field Trip to Bowling Alley	16 Father's Day Picnic	17 Garrett 3rd Birthday
18 Weekly Theme: "Don't bug me!"	19 Saftey Drill Week	20	21 Summer Camp Sleep Out!	22 Brianne 2nd Birthday	23	24 James 1st Birthday
25 Weekly Theme: Under the Big Top	26 Lindsey 3rd Birthday	27 Preschool Field Trip to the Zoo	28 Be a clown day!	29 Parent's Round Table 7:00 pm	30 Lemonade & Cookie Sale	

FIGURE 3–18 Center Calendar

example of a birthday board can be found on Figure 3–20. It is important to note if you have children from religious backgrounds, such as families who are practicing Jehovah Witnesses, who do not observe the celebrations of birthdays or of most holidays. Know your families and be sensitive to their beliefs.

THE WEATHER BOARD

Weather is a perfect medium to explore with the children on a daily basis. It provides many opportunities for discussions and teachable moments. The weather chart example in Figure 3–21 is just one example of how to structure a weather corner. Hang the chart at a level the children can observe and interact with the chart. Explore the weather board with the children when they arrive in the morning or return from outdoor play so they can easily recall the type of weather they recently experienced. Discuss the different types

CLASS NEWSLETTER

Enriching the Lives of Children Since 1979

HIGHLIGHTS

OUR MONTHLY NEWSLETTER
FOR JUNE

> ## MS. PARISH
> ## SPOTLIGHT TEACHER OF THE YEAR
> ## PURPLE GRAPES TEACHER

Dear Families,

    We are pleased to announce Mrs. Laura has been voted our "Teacher of the Year." Thank you for your participation. With such a fine teaching staff, it was a tough decision. We are proud of Laura and appreciate all of her contributions over the past six years. Here are some of the comments you and the children shared with us.

Sincerely,
Helen, Director

Miss Laura is always friendly, patient, understanding and kind. She is very willing to listen to both child and parent comments and concerns. She also shows a great concern for the children's welfare.

                    The Pecks Family

She's the best. Her rapport with the children is exactly what every mother hopes for. She treats all the children the same with interest in what they all have to say. Her smile is contagious. It makes you forget you're hurried, sometimes frantic morning or day at work. She's the kind of teacher I hope you would look for when hiring all caregivers and teachers.

                    The Happy family

We have never heard her be cross with a child. She puts interesting things in the room to brighten it up. She writes exciting lesson plans and gets the children to discuss things! She always seems to have a smile on her face for the children. She shows them they are important by focusing on them and listening to what they have to say. We think she is great!

                    Mrs. Esther Parent

P.S. I feel good about having her with Collin when I can't be.

Miss Laura is....
1. always cheerful
2. great with the children
3. a good motivator
4. very helpful
5. very loving

She also gives out delicious great snacks and has a great smile.

                    "Peter" & Mr. Jake Father

To Miss Laura,

We are so glad you are "teacher of the year." You definitely deserve this honor. I love to come to school each day because you make learning fun. You are kind and caring and a wonderful teacher. Thank you for being great. Mommy thinks so too!

                    Love, Mikey

Harry really likes Miss Laura because she loves airplanes as much as Harry does.
The John Doe Family

FIGURE 3–19 Class Newsletter

FIGURE 3–20 Birthday Bulletin Board

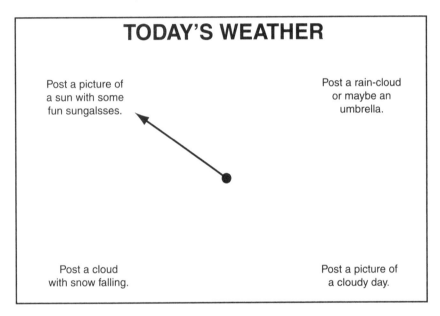

FIGURE 3–21 Today's Weather Board

of clothing they wear to match the weather they experienced. In some regions of the country weather patterns do not change as often as in others. Offer plenty of pictures depicting different types of weather as a point of discussion with the children.

NOTES HOME / STAFF COLLABORATION

The director is responsible for the overall well-being of the staff, parents, and children. The director must be kept informed with regard to any unusual changes, challenges, or problems that may occur during the course of the shift. It can be very disconcerting for an emotionally upset client to approach a director who is completely uninformed. Prior to sending notes home, discuss any written communication with the director other than requested personal supplies or each child's daily record. After discussing the problem together, you can devise a shared plan of action. Sharing your concerns with the director will allow problem solving as well as keep him or her continuously informed. The director has encountered many of these situations before and often has workable solutions that will be beneficial to all.

FRAGILE PARENT RELATIONSHIPS

Experienced early care and education professionals are well aware that newly enrolled families are most "fragile" during the first several weeks of their child's attendance. This is the first time some parents have been separated from their child for any length of time. They may experience sadness, anxiety, and for some, feelings of guilt. This is a hand-holding stage as a trusting relationship is established. It is human nature, once we become familiar with our routines, to easily forget how it feels to be "brand new" to the center setting. Challenge yourself to look at each "new" family and recollect how it felt on your first day.

For a successful liaison, it is crucial to establish trust and rapport quickly. Not only is it important to greet each child and family member every day on arrival, but it is also helpful to provide an extra-big welcome in the morning to families new to your program. They will appreciate efforts on behalf of the staff to include them in discussions while establishing care for their children. Show them where to store their child's belongings, where to sign in for the day, and where they can find the child's daily sheets. Learn the correct spelling and pronunciation of their names and the name of their child. Offer them information about the daily routines, or invite them to visit before their first day. Introduce them to other parents so they begin to feel a part of the group quickly. As rapport builds, a level of trust will begin to develop and they will naturally settle into a familiar, comfortable routine. Then it will become easier for the parents to move in and out when they drop their little one off.

Other times a client might be considered fragile usually revolve around an upsetting situation involving the child. If they do not feel their concerns are viewed as legitimate by the staff, their trust is compromised. For example, some fairly common scenarios could involve their recently healthy child now experiencing frequent illnesses, or their child's relationship with another child such as biting. Again, this is a time to make extra effort to reassure the parents that you are very committed and sympathetic to their concerns. Share more information to assist their understanding. If a situation can be improved, outline what plan of action you have put into place to correct the situation or prevent the incident from recurring.

Sometimes parental concerns do not involve classroom situations. For example, there may be an error with their billing or how their billing has been handled. Because parents naturally bond with classroom teachers through positive daily contact, sometimes they feel more comfortable sharing their concerns with the classroom personnel rather than with administrative personnel. At times they may experience some dissatisfaction in other center matters. If you hear consistently a parent voicing a concern, it is very helpful to share these observations with the director. Doing so provides an opportunity to proactively alleviate any misunderstandings or frustrations the client may be experiencing. It takes a whole team to make early care a pleasant and positive experience for everyone, and it is very important to keep the lines of communication open on all levels. With the center managers' wide experience, matters can often be smoothed out and mutually acceptable outcomes reached quickly.

REFERENCES

Kostelnik, M., Soderman, A., & Whiren, A. (1993). *Developmentally appropriate programs in early childhood education.* New York: Merrill.

RECOMMENDED RESOURCES

American Academy of Pediatrics, S. P. Shelov and R. E. Hannemann. *Caring for Your Baby and young child: Birth to age 5.* Retrieved from http://www.aap.org

Caring for Our Children National Health & Safety Performance Standards (2nd ed.) http://www.ncr.ed

High/Scope Educational Research Foundation, http://www.highscope.org

Jurek, D. (1995). *Teaching young children.* Fearon Teacher Aids.

Marhoefer, P. E., & Vadnais, L. A. (1988). *Caring for the developing child.* Clifton Park, NY: Thomson Delmar Learning.

To find your specific
State's Licensing, Rules
and Regulations go to:

http://nrc.uchsc.edu

Hygiene, Cleaning, and Disinfecting

Proper cleaning, disinfecting, and hygiene practices employed consistently in an early care and education environment significantly reduce the spread of infection and disease. Disinfecting and cleaning are two distinctly different procedures used to reduce or prevent the spread of germs and require their own specific measures to achieve the intended results. *Cleaning* is a *less* rigorous procedure and is designed to remove dirt, soil, and small amounts of bacteria. It *does not eliminate all germs*. Soap, detergents, and cleaners are examples of cleaning products. *Disinfecting* procedures are *more rigorous* and refer to cleaning surfaces with the use of chemicals, *virtually eliminating all germs*. For a disinfectant solution to work effectively, the instructions must be followed exactly. Disinfecting products require a certain concentration of solution and must remain in contact with the contaminated item for a specific period of time. The Environmental Protection Agency (EPA) regulates the use of disinfectants. To avoid confusing a cleaning agent with a disinfecting agent, read the label. Products with properties capable of disinfecting will bear an EPA approval on the label.

If you are mixing your own disinfecting solutions, the National Health and Safety Performance Standards for Child Care recommends ¼ cup of bleach in 1 gallon of water. Mix fresh daily. To avoid creating a poisonous gas, never mix bleach with anything other than water. After cleaning the item with soap and water, spray with the bleach solution until it glistens and leave it on at least 2 minutes before wiping with a paper towel.

Chlorine bleach solutions may aggravate asthma or other respiratory conditions. Some care providers are concerned with the potential toxic effects of common household products used abundantly in an early care environment. There are several effective natural disinfecting products on the market. Check your local health food stores for a variety of products currently available, or check in the Recommended Resources section at the end of this chapter.

STORING PERSONAL BELONGINGS / SANITATION STORAGE

Provide each child with an individual container or cubby locker to store book bags, clothing, hats, coats, and all other personal items. Do not let one child's personal belongings touch another child's. This habit will reduce the potential cross-contamination of other children's personal items, from germs or infestation, caused by contagious conditions such as head lice (pediculosis) or scabies, to name a few.

WET AND SOILED CLOTHING

When the child's clothing becomes wet or soiled, remove the soiled item and replace it with something clean and dry. Secure the soiled article of clothing in a plastic bag, and store it in a place for the parents to find at the time of departure. To ensure clothing is not damaged or misplaced, do not launder. Each parent has his or her own personal way of laundering clothing. To avoid mildewed clothing or permanent stains, send home promptly.

HAND-WASHING PROCEDURES

Frequent hand washing is a cornerstone for a healthy early care and education program. Proper hand washing prevents the spread of many communicable diseases such as *E. coli* contamination (found largely in feces), hepatitis, giardia, pinworms, and a host of many more common ailments. All are spread through a fecal–oral route (anus to mouth). Giardiasis and pinworms are the two most common parasitic infections among children in the United States. Wong (1999) found that "the incidence of intestinal parasitic disease, especially giardiasis, has increased among young children who attend daycare centers" (p. 736). And Wong says, "Hand washing is the single most effective and critical measure and control of hepatitis in any setting" (p. 1577).

The best defense for reducing the spread of illness lies in consistent hand washing habits. The following list recommends hand washing procedures (Figure 4–1) for staff and children: Use these procedures before and after playing in the sand and water table, after playing with pets, after play outdoors, before and after preparing bottles or serving food, before and after diapering or toileting, before and after administering first aid, before and after giving medication, before working with children and at the end of the

---

Posted Hand Washing Procedures

1	Turn on warm water* and adjust to comfortable temperature.	2	Wet hands and apply soap.	3	Wash vigorously for approximately 10–20 seconds.
4	Dry hands with paper towel.	5	Turn off faucet with paper towel.	6	Dispose of paper towel in a lidded trash receptacle with a plastic liner.

Use hand washing procedures for staff and children

- before and after preparing bottles or serving food.
- before and after diapering or toileting.
- before and after administering first aid.
- before and after giving medication.
- before working with the children and at the end of the day.
- before leaving the classroom for a break.
- after wiping nose discharge, coughing, or sneezing.
- before and after playing in the sand and water table.
- after playing with pets.
- after playing outdoors.

*Some states require cold water for children's hand washing sinks. Check your state for specific guidelines.

FIGURE 4–1 Posted Hand Washing Procedures

day, before leaving the classroom for a break, and after wiping a nose discharge, coughing, or sneezing. Check with your local licensing agency for any other requirements listed in your area.

Install liquid soap with a pump or a dispenser and disposable paper towels near the sink. These aids are an integral part of hand washing. The National Center for Infectious Diseases (2005) encourages us to turn on the warm water (not more than 103° F) and adjust accordingly to achieve a comfortable temperature. Some states require the use of cold water only for children's hand-washing sinks; check your state for specific guidelines. Wet hands and apply liquid soap. Rub hands vigorously for approximately 10 to 20 seconds. The soap, combined with the scrubbing action, helps dislodge and remove germs. Rinse hands well, and dry hands with a clean disposable paper towel. Use a disposable paper towel to turn off the faucet and to avoid recontamination of your clean hands. Dispose of the paper towel in a lidded trash receptacle lined with a plastic liner. A trash can operated with a foot mechanism is an expensive option, yet the hand-free action reduces the possibility of recontamination of clean hands.

Install sinks with running hot (regulated by an antiscald device) and cold water, installed at the children's height to promote frequent use. Disinfect toilet seats, water fountains with 10% solution bleach: water ratio (1 part chlorine bleach to 10 parts water) or any registered EPA disinfectant prepared according to instructions. Registered EPA approval is placed on the product label.

EMPLOYING UNIVERSAL PRECAUTIONS AND THE PROPER USE OF GLOVES

In 1991 OSHA (Occupational Safety and Health Administration) established a standard for blood-borne pathogens, mandating that measures to protect employees from exposure to potentially infectious blood pathogens were necessary. Hepatitis B (HBV) and human immunodeficiency virus (HIV) are the two most common sources of blood-borne pathogens. HBV is a disease of the liver contracted by exposure to contaminated blood. It causes inflammation and destruction of the liver and, if not cured, eventually leads to death. HIV is a disease contracted through contaminated body fluids, and has the potential to lead to AIDS, which destroys the human immune system.

Center staff members are commonly exposed to body fluids in the form of urine, feces, vomitus, sweat, saliva, breast milk, and nasal secretions. It is difficult to stress the importance of using universal precautions without sounding a fear alarm. Contracting a case of HIV/AIDS is highly unlikely. Kinnell reports the Centers for Disease Control and Prevention stated, "We have never documented a case of HIV being transmitted through biting" (p. 54). Because it is impossible to know when a person is infected with such a disease, *all* body fluids or secretions *must* be treated as if they were infected with disease.

If exposure to another person's body fluids may occur, put on a pair of disposable, moisture-proof gloves before making contact with the contaminated source. Place gloves in several convenient areas of the classroom so they can be retrieved at a moment's notice. To avoid contaminating yourself with soiled gloves, remove them properly. Instructions for proper gloving procedures are given in Figure 4–2. Post this next to the First Aid Directives for a quick reference. Follow your company's policies for disposal of contaminated supplies and equipment.

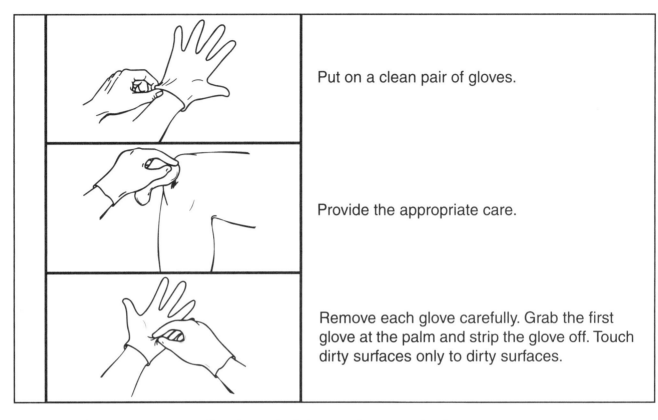

Put on a clean pair of gloves.

Provide the appropriate care.

Remove each glove carefully. Grab the first glove at the palm and strip the glove off. Touch dirty surfaces only to dirty surfaces.

FIGURE 4–2 Gloving Procedures (See Appendix C for complete procedure)

DENTAL HYGIENE

The Centers for Disease Control and Prevention offer several recommendations for tooth care for young children. It recommends beginning to clean teeth early using a small, soft toothbrush. Three-year-olds are capable of brushing their teeth with supervision. Only use a small-pea size amount of toothpaste. Teach the children to spit out and rinse after brushing. The toothbrushes need to be stored in a properly ventilated individual container, labeled with each child's name. In some states the toothbrushes are to be stored so they can air-dry. To avoid cross-contamination, the brushes should not touch each other. Discard and replace the toothbrush each time a child experiences a serious cold, flu, vomiting, fever, or other communicable disease, to avoid a cycle of recontamination. Children need to brush at least twice a day. Involve the parents when planning a schedule. It might be more feasible to have their child brush in the morning before they come and in the evening after their family dinner. The center staff could promote positive oral care habits by providing water for the children to rinse after eating. Refer to the American Dental Association (ADA) at http://www.ada.org (Web site) to find helpful information to share with the children's family that promotes positive dental hygiene habits.

CLEANING THE LEARNING MATERIALS AND EQUIPMENT

A great deal of activity occurs in an early care and teaching environment. The equipment and learning materials are handled by many little hands every day. Establishing regular cleaning routines that employ general hygiene practices can reduce the spread of germs and infectious diseases. Before disinfecting, wash the surface of soiled equipment, such as tables, chairs, and learning materials with soap and water. As your final step, disinfect with a sanitizing solution. If you are using bleach as your disinfecting agent, then use ¼ cup of bleach to one gallon of water on the surface for a minimum of 2 minutes. It is best to allow items to air-dry. The same process applies to learning materials unless you are soaking them. Aronson and Spahr (2002) note, "If you are using bleach and a soaking method to sanitize learning materials, use a more concentrated solution, because each object can introduce germs into the solution. The recommended solution of household bleach for soaking learning materials is ¾ cup of bleach to 1 gallon of water. Put learning materials into a net bag, soak them for 5 minutes, rinse with water, and hang the bag to air-dry" (p. 16). Once the learning materials have completely dried, they are ready for use again!

REFERENCES

Aronson, S. S., & Spahr, P. M. (2002). *Healthy young children.* Washington, DC: National Association for the Education of Young Children.

Kimel, G. (2002). *No biting.* St. Paul, MN: Redleaf Press.

National Association of Child Care Professionals and National Accreditation Commission. (2005). *Washing Hands,* http://www.naccp.org.

National Center for Infectious Diseases. (2005) *An ounce of prevention: Keeps the germs away—hand washing procedure.* Information Sheet. Retrieved March 8, 2005, from http://www.cdc.gov/ncidod/op/handwashing.html.

Wong, P. D. (1999). *Whaley & Wong's, care of infants and children,* St. Louis, MSO: Mosby.

RECOMMENDED RESOURCES

American Dental Association (ADA). http://www.ada.org.

Church, D. S. (2004). *The MELALEUCA Wellness Guide (8th edition).* Littleton, CO: RM Barry Publications.

Health

To find your specific
State's Licensing, Rules
and Regulations go to:

http://nrc.uchsc.edu

SICK BAY AND ISOLATION AREA

Centers need to prepare a sick bay and an isolation area for a sick child to rest until their parent or guardian can call for them. Equip a space or room (depending on state regulations) with a bed or cot and a crib in an area where constant supervision can be administered. Sometimes space is very limited, and a cot in the director's office will have to suffice. If a bed is used, provide several changes of linens for individual use only. Select a variety of learning materials and books to offer the children until their departure. Provide a thermometer to measure body temperatures and a container large enough to catch emesis, in case the child vomits. Place a child-size chair in the area for the child while you administer first aid. It will be most convenient to locate the locked medication/first aid cabinet and a small refrigerator nearby, stocked with a container and lid labeled "refrigerated medications only," ice in plastic bags or cold packs, popsicles (for mouth and lip injuries), juice boxes, and fresh drinking water. Place the key on a hook nearby out of children's reach.

FIRST AID CABINET AND FIRST AID KITS

Minor injuries are common in a center setting. Children will experience scratches and bumps as they go about their activities of daily living. Prepare a first aid cabinet and kits to use in the event of an accident. Provide a first aid cabinet near the sick bay area used to isolate sick children. The first aid cabinet must remain locked (place the key on a hook out of reach of the children) at all times so it is not accessible to the children but is accessible to the staff in a moment's notice. If your center transports, then place a complete first aid kit in the vehicle. Stock the first aid cabinet with:

- Disposable nonporous gloves
- American Red Cross first aid manual or American Academy of Pediatrics (AAP) standard first aid chart or an equivalent first aid guide
- Nonglass thermometer
- Bandages
- Band-aids or similar products
- Sterile gauze pads
- Triangular cloth splint
- Plastic splint for immobilizing a limb
- Scissors
- Tweezers

- Safety pins
- Adhesive strips
- Disposable apron
- Protective glasses
- Pocket mouth-to-mouth resuscitation mask to open an airway

Syrup of ipecac has been used in centers in the past to induce vomiting. However, causing vomiting when a caustic or corrosive substance has been swallowed can cause irreversible physical damage. For this reason, best practices no longer recommends the use of syrup of ipecac in child care facilities. Provide a source for running water and soap near the first aid station to cleanse wounds. If running water is not available on a field trip, use a waterless antiseptic hand cleaner.

The playground is another area to provide a convenient source of first aid supplies. Some centers find it convenient to hang a fanny pack in each classroom near the door so the teacher can wear it on the playground; use it in the classroom for minor injuries, on the playground, and on field trips. Because accidents on the playground often involve blood, the teacher will need to immediately employ universal precautions before handling the child. If a fanny pack is not used, another option on the playground involves installing a mailbox on a post. Stock the mailbox with items such as:

- Waterless antiseptic hand cleaner
- Disposable nonporous gloves
- Tissues
- Wipes
- Plastic trash bags
- Sterile gauze pads
- Band-aids or similar product

All items contaminated with blood should be placed in plastic bags. These materials should be handled according to your center's policy.

MANAGING MEDICATIONS

Administering medications in a center is common and requires special attention to detail. In some states all personnel distributing medication must take a special class and earn a certification. Check your local regulations for your area mandates. Instruct all personnel to always wash their hands before beginning, make sure they have the correct child by name and match it to the label on the prescription. Double-check the proper dose. Always use a medication spoon or measuring spoon to be certain the proper dosage is administered. Check the expiration date on the label. To avoid a visit to the doctor, sometimes families attempt to self-medicate their children and reuse medication that is outdated. Follow the instructions for how frequently it should be given and if it should be given before or after eating. Once the medication is given, document it on the Daily Medication sheet (example in Figure 5–1). Details for using the Daily Medication records are explained further later on.

Medications prescribed for an individual child should be kept in the original container bearing the original pharmacy label showing the prescription number, the date it was filled, the physician's name, directions for use, and the child's name. Send medication home every day with the child. If the child needs a repeat dosage the following day, begin

Daily Medication Sheet

Child's Name	RX Number & Type of Medication	Amount & Route Administered	Date	Time	Given By: First Name	Last Name
Camela (Enter Last Name)	RX 652201 Amoxicillin 250 Milligrams	1 tsp by mouth	02-22	11:00 am	Mrs.	Hoffriah
				5:00pm	Ms.	Szalay

FIGURE 5–1 Daily Medication Sheet

with fresh instructions and do not rely on information from the previous day. For the protection of the child and yourself, do not give any over-the-counter medications unless directed in writing from the child's physician and their family. Check your local regulations for mandates governing over-the-counter medication usage.

Occasionally a child develops symptoms of illness such as high fevers, persistent cough, or ear pain caused by an infection. Although most programs are not equipped to provide continuous sick care, there often is a lapse in time before the parent/guardian can arrive to attend to the ill child. It takes time to locate working parents, especially if they are out in "the field." Sometimes they are delayed waiting for a suitable replacement at their place of work—for example, a nurse or firefighter. Before this happens, collect presigned, physician-approved orders for fever-reducing medications using the Medical Authorization for Nonprescription Medications template found in the Forms and Templates Appendix (example in Figure 5–2). Give medications only with this pre-approved authorization and under the directions of the parents in writing. Again, this is an area that is regulated differently in many states, so check your local regulating agency for guidance.

Use the Daily Medication sheet to document the administration of medications throughout the day. It includes the date, child's name, the type of medication, how much medication should be administered, the route of administration (such as by mouth, in the eyes, ears, or rectum), and how often to repeat it. To maintain an accurate medication history, sign the record with your full name and the time it is administered. Store all medications requiring refrigeration in a container with a secure lid labeled "Refrigerated medications only." In a locked cabinet that is inaccessible to the children, store any medications that do not require refrigeration. Store the preapproved authorizations where there is easy access,

Medical Authorization
for Nonprescription Medication*

Name of Child: _____ *Jessie (Enter Last Name)* _____   Date: _____ *09-18-2009* _____

The staff is authorized to dispense the following medications as ordered by your physician and directed by the parents/guardian.

Please indicate specific medication, route it is to be given, dosage, and frequency.

Type	Medication	Route	Dosage	Frequency
Nonaspirin Preparation	Tylenol	By mouth	0.4cc	Every 4 hours over 101° as needed Send Home
Aspirin Preparation				
Cough Preparation	Robitussin	By mouth	1/2 tsp	Every 6 hours for persistent cough
Decongestant				
Skin Ointment	Desitin	On perineum	Thin layer	Every diaper chenge when redness develops
Diaper Wipes	Any brand	As directed		As needed
Sunscreen	Any brand	On skin	Small amount	Before outdoor play

_____ *Dr. John* _____   _____ *Dr. John* _____   _____ *XXX-XXX-XXXX* _____
Print Name of Physician   Signature of Physician   Phone Number

_____ *Mr. Collin* _____
Parent/Guardian Signature

* Complete this form on admission and update annually. Store medical authorizations in an index box and place in or near locked cabinet for quick referencing.

FIGURE 5–2 Medical Authorization for Nonprescription Medication

such as the locked medicine cabinet or in a file box nearby. Place the Daily Medication record near Spread the Word as discussed in Chapter 7, "Facilitating Three-Year-Olds and Their Families" or check your center's policies for directions where to most conveniently locate these documents for the families.

Because many medications such as cough suppressants, antihistamines, and expectorants are required every 4 to 6 hours, or on schedules three times a day or four times a day, create a schedule to administer most medications at specific times. Specifying what times medications are usually administered encourages the parents to pick a schedule that makes sense for the center and simultaneously adheres to a proper time regiment advised for medications. Encourage the parents to administer the first dose in the morning before arriving. Mornings typically are very busy, and the center staff is occupied with so many details already that a medication dosage could easily be missed. Also, it is not uncommon for the amount of children on medications to increase substantially during the winter months. Suggest the center can be responsible for the midday dose administered typically around lunchtime and again around 4 or 5 PM, leaving the evening dose for the parents to administer. Adjust the times if you are open nontraditional hours. Most antibiotics for children can now be administered twice a day or every 10 to 12 hours, therefore doses need not be administered during the day. There will always be occasional exceptions to the scheduled times, such as a sudden need for an asthma treatment. Scheduling most medications to be given at the same time decreases the risk of missing treatments and doses and increases the accuracy of administration. Some states require that only one person administer medications and that person must receive specific training before assuming that responsibility.

On a final note, if your program provides care for infants, for a myriad of reasons infant medication schedules are better served by providing the infant room a separate Daily Medication record. Infant schedules for eating and sleeping are quite different from those of the other age groups. Unless you have a very small number of children in your program, separate the infants' Daily Medication record from the three-year-old through school-age Daily Medication record.

MEASURING BODY TEMPERATURES

If you suspect a child is too warm or has an elevated temperature, measure and record the body temperature. The safest method for recording a child's temperature is under the arm (also known as an axillary temperature). The average normal temperature for an axillary temperature is 97.4°F or 36.3°C. If you are using a plastic (nonglass) thermometer, be sure to shake the mercury reading below 98°F before measuring the body temperature. Hold the thermometer under the child's arm for 10 minutes. Mercury is extremely toxic and can cause a high risk hazard if the thermometer is broken and it escapes. If that ever occurs, call Poison Control to receive specific instructions. To save time and provide convenience, many centers opt for a more expensive route and use thermometer strips for the forehead or electronic thermometers. If you use an electronic thermometer, hold it in place until you hear a beeping sound.

Report an elevated body temperature and initiate an illness report immediately, and notify the attending supervisor so the parents/guardians can be contacted. Record the child's temperature reading on a Suggested Illness record (example in Figure 5–3). Continue checking the temperature every one half hour to monitor any drastic changes. Children who have elevated temperatures must not come back to the group for 24 hours after the return to a normal range unless advised differently by the family's physician.

SUGGESTED ILLNESS

Child's name: ___Courtney (Enter Last Name)___   Date: _____10/04/05_____

SYMPTOMS ARE:

___102° F___   Body Temperature (under arm, add 1 degree)

_____   Vomiting

_____   Diarrhea

_____   Exhibiting signs of a communicable illness

_____   Skin condition requiring further treatment

Other: _____Complaining her left ear hurts_____

Report initiated by: _____Mr. Anthony_____

Were parents notified? Yes __✓__ No _____ By whom? _Ms. Denise_

Time parents notified: 1st Attempt _1:30 pm_   _____Dad_____
                                                     Which Parent Notified

                         2nd Attempt _1:35 pm_   _____Mom_____
                                                     Which Parent Notified

                         3rd Attempt _____   _____
                                                     Which Parent Notified

Time child departed: ___1:50 pm___

Director's signature: _____Mrs. Helen_____

Children exhibiting a temperature that exceeds 100°F, symptoms of vomiting (1–3 forceful rushes), diarrhea (defined as watery, mucous, foul-smelling bowel movement), or an unrecognized rash shall not return to group care for a minimum of 24 hours after treatment or before symptoms subside.

1. Office Copy   2. Parent/Guardian Copy

FIGURE 5–3 Suggested Illness Report

IMMUNIZATIONS

To protect all children attending the center, medical authorities mandate that all children have current immunizations. Because the recommended dosages and types of immunizations continually fluctuate and differ from state to state, you can refer to the American Academy of Pediatrics Web site at http://www.aap.org for the most recent schedule, or contact your local department of health. Sometimes a center encounters children who do not have current immunizations for a variety of reasons, such as medical conditions or religious preferences. If immunizations are withheld for either such reason, collect in writing from the parent/legal guardian, the child's physician, and/or religious leader with the specific reason, and keep it in the child's record. Special care should be taken to notify and exclude underimmunized children from the program if an active vaccine-preventable disease occurs in the facility.

ALLERGIES AND POSTING ALLERGY NOTICES

Allergies are caused by a variety of substances known as allergens. Some can be triggered by a range of substances, which include venom, toxins, nuts, latex, various drugs, stings, pollen, dust, mold, animal dander, and shellfish. A severe reaction can occur quickly, usually within a few minutes. Severe reactions are usually dramatic, with symptoms such as swelling on the face; tight, difficult breathing; and hives that look like red, rashy, blotches on the skin. Mild allergic reactions are more common than the severe ones. Mild allergic reactions display the same symptoms as severe reactions, but in much weaker forms and take longer to develop. Local reactions such as swelling of an entire arm or leg can be severe but are not commonly lethal. If an allergy is severe, recommend that the child wear a Medic Alert bracelet for immediate identification of the allergen if an exposure ever occurs. Severe reactions can be life threatening. Anaphylactic shock will very quickly interfere with the child's ability to breathe. If a child or staff member with a known anaphylactic shock history is in attendance at the center, then a kit for epinephrine injections (with parental and physician instructions for staff usage) should always be kept on the premises and should follow the person on excursions. If the child is exposed to a known allergen or begins to exhibit signs of a severe reaction, call 911 or other appropriate number. Milder reactions, although not life threatening, also require a doctor's care, especially if the reaction has not occurred before.

The KIDEX Individual Monthly Profile and Introduce Us to Your Three-Year-Old forms provide a space for listing and recording any allergies a child may have. Always post a list of all children and their known allergies and in the KIDEX Class Book.

ILLNESS RECORDS AND ILLNESS-TRACKING REPORTS

Begin each day with a general health assessment of each child. Familiarity with each child will help you become a reliable detector of unusual physical symptoms. If a child has a preexisting medical condition or a physical handicap, become familiar with their particular needs.

Minor illnesses are often marked by a change in their general appearance or behavior such as glassy eyes, flushed cheeks, swollen glands, or sluggish movements. Remove and isolate sick children from the group if they have a temperature over 100°F, symptoms of vomiting (1 to 3 forceful rushes), diarrhea (defined as watery, mucous, foul-smelling bowel movement), or an

Illness Tracking Report

Name of Child	Time	Type of Illness	Person Reporting Illness	Director Notified	Report Filed	Parent Notified	Time Called
Emily (Enter Last Name)	12:30 pm	Fever 101°F	Ms. Caroline	✓	✓	✓	1:30 pm
Jaden (Enter Last Name)	11:00 am	Diarrhea	Mrs. Michelle	✓	✓	✓	11:15 am
Olivia (Enter Last Name)	2:00 pm	Vomiting	Mr. Walter	✓	✓	✓	2:30 pm
Marta (Enter Last Name)	7:30 am	Earache	Mrs. Donna	✓	✓	✓	8:00 am
Chen (Enter Last Name)	8:15 am	Headache	Ms. Ellen	✓	✓	✓	8:45 am
Joshua (Enter Last Name)	4:00 pm	Split lip	Mr. Thomas	✓	✓	✓	4:30 pm
Andrew (Enter Last Name)	4:30 pm	Fever 100°F	Ms. Regina	✓	✓	✓	4:45 pm

FIGURE 5–4 Illness Tracking Report

undiagnosed rash. If you suspect a child is exhibiting any of these symptoms, then complete an illness report with details and give to the director to initiate the next step. Once the director confirms the child is sick, then take action to notify the child's parents.

Families often feel frustration, guilt, and anxiety about missing work and having a sick child. Be sure the child is ill before disturbing the family. If at any time a child is exposed to a communicable illness such as chicken pox, measles, etc., then post a notice on the Current Events Bulletin Board for proper notification. Descriptions for common communicable illnesses and symptoms can be found in Chapter 7 and in the other KIDEX book series for children under the age of 5.

Pediatricians appreciate written documentation accompanying a sick child who has just arrived from the center. All too often families arrive at the office an examination with little or no information regarding the symptoms the child has been experiencing. Provide the family a copy of the Suggested Illness report so they will have details in hand about the symptoms to take with them to the physician. Track reports of illnesses on a daily basis to help identify potential outbreak patterns that may be developing in the center (example in Figure 5–4).

HOW TO PREVENT AND HANDLE A HEAD LICE INFESTATION

Whenever children are cared for in groups, head lice infestation is possible. Children with head lice infestation usually have older siblings that attend elementary school and unsuspectingly carry lice home to their family. Head lice are a potential problem, but do *not* indicate a family is dirty. Head lice can be picked up anywhere, such as in movie theaters or from the back of a bus seat or airline seat.

To reduce the possibility of a head lice epidemic in your center, the program needs to be proactive and to conduct weekly head checks for every child. Figure 5–5 is an example of a completed Head Lice Checklist. To include all children, especially those with a part-time schedule, head checks need to occur on a different day each week. Plan to administer head checks right after a nap period when hair brushing, combing, and grooming are already occurring. It takes very little time and can be accomplished very quickly and efficiently. Make sure you are in a well-lit area. You may see a louse but they move very quickly, and you may only detect their eggs (nits). As you comb the hair, observe the hair roots for any little nits, which are the eggs. They often attach about ¼ to ½ inch from the hair root. They are very tiny and translucent, and you can sometimes see through them. It is easy to distinguish between a nit and a scalp flake: A nit will not move very easily, because it is more firmly attached than a hair flake.

A head louse does not live very long without a warm-blooded host, in this case human beings. For head lice to survive, they must obtain their source of nutrition from their host. Head lice infestation can be treated by using special shampoos formulated to destroy the live nits and their eggs. Check with your local pharmacist for other similar recommendations. Send all the childrens' bedding home with the families.

If you discover a child with a potential problem, contact the parent immediately and isolate the child from other children until the child departs. Send home all of the children's

Head Lice Checklist

Group Name: _____The Peaches_____

Name	Sunday	Monday	Tuesday	Wednesday	Thursday	Friday	Saturday
		April 29	May 1	May 10	May 18	May 21	
Baily (Enter Last Name)		A	C	C	A	A	
Emily (Enter Last Name)		C	C	C	C	C	
Jared (Enter Last Name)		C	C	C	C	C	
Jenni (Enter Last Name)		C	C	A	C	C	
Mary (Enter Last Name)		C	C	C	C	C	
Robert (Enter Last Name)		C	C	C	C	C	
Kellie (Enter Last Name)		C	A	C	C	C	
Erin (Enter Last Name)		C	C	C	C	C	
Ian (Enter Last Name)		C	C	C	C	C	
Tamika (Enter Last Name)		C	C	C	A	C	
Natosha (Enter Last Name)		C	C	C	C	C	
Mitch (Enter Last Name)		C	C	C	C	C	
Harry (Enter Last Name)		C	C	C	C	C	

C = Clear   **A = Absent**   **P = Possible**

(**Reminder:** Please check weekly on different days of the week.)

FIGURE 5–5 Head Lice Checklist

blankets, soft learning materials, pillows, hats, coats, or any other personal items that might harbor head lice or their eggs. Clean or bag all items the child has come in contact with, such as dressup clothing or pillows in the reading area. Instruct the families to launder all washable items in hot water and dry them at a high heat for at least 20 minutes. Unwashable items can be bagged in plastic trash bags and left for a week or so before using them again, or sprays are available for delousing if a quicker turnaround is needed, such as for a favorite stuffed bunny. Establish a "no nit policy": do not allow the infested child to return to the program until all evidence of nits have been removed from the child's hair. To prevent the spread of head lice and reduce the possibility of an epidemic, check every child's head for the next five days past the last discovery.

Cross-contamination of lice can be a challenge if measures are not employed to separate personal items such as combs and hairbrushes. It is tempting to discourage children from bringing combs and brushes to the center. Yet positive opportunities to interact with each child during grooming far outweigh the measures required to reduce such occurrences. The children need to be touched in positive ways during the day and hair brushing and combing is a wonderful way to do this. Separate and store hair items in individual closed containers. Plastic zippered bags available at the grocery store are inexpensive and work very well. Label each storage container, comb, and brush with the child's name.

A diligent effort to maintain stringent hygienic practices and regular head checks will thwart the possibility of an epidemic in your program.

RECOMMENDED RESOURCES

Aronson S. S., & T. R. Shope. *Managing infectious diseases in child care and schools*. Elk Grove, IL: American Academy of Pediatrics Health and Safety Tips.

Health and Safety Tips. *Daily health checks*. Retrieved February 6, 2005, from http://www.nrc.uchsc.edu.

Health and Safety Tips, *Medication administration in the child care setting*. Retrieved February 11, 2005, from http://www.nrc.uchsc.edu

Immunizations. Retrieved March 11, 2005, from http://www.nrc.uchsc.edu.

Kemper, K. J. (1996). *The holistic pediatrician*. New York: HarperCollins.

PLACES TO PURCHASE FIRST AID SUPPLIES

Child Care Workers Compliance Guidelines for the OSHA Blood-borne Pathogen Standard. Professional Medical Enterprises, 450 Bedford Street, Lexington, MA 02173

Coastal Training Company, Coastal Video Communications Corp., 3083 Brickhouse Court, Virginia Beach, VA 23452 *Fax:* 1-804-498-3657. *Info:*1-800-767-7703. http://www.coastal.com.

Coney Safety Products, 3202 Lathem Dr., Madison, WI 53713; 1-800-356-9100

CHAPTER

6

Safety

To find your specific
State's Licensing, Rules
and Regulations go to:

http://nrc.uchsc.edu

POSTING FIRST AID DIRECTIVES

Early care and education professionals who are adequately trained in cardiopulmonary resuscitation (CPR), artificial respiration, and first aid procedures, specifically for infant and children rescue, are an asset to the children and to the program. It is advisable for all child care personnel to receive and maintain current CPR certification, artificial respiration, first aid training, and universal precautions with regard to handling body fluids.

Post first aid and choking directives in each room to serve as a quick reminder what steps to follow in case of an emergency. First aid directives are a brief review of what to do if an emergency does occur. There are many different emergencies. Figure 6–1 outlines some of the most common emergencies, such as poisoning, bleeding, choking, convulsions, shock, nosebleeds, and situations requiring artificial respiration. Emergency numbers for the poison control center, fire department, emergency help, medical and dental help, ambulance, and the police station must be placed next to each phone. Write the center address and major cross street on the phone list. If a need to click or dial a specific number is necessary to set a telephone outside line, include that as part of the emergency number. Pertinent information that is readily available during an emergency situation can provide the calm needed for staff to perform at an optimum level.

LEAVING THE ROOM UNATTENDED

Child/adult ratios are established and maintained for classroom safety. Whenever an adult leaves the classroom environment and the number of children remains the same, an unsafe ratio is created. A room with children present should *never* be left unattended by an adult! Leaving children unattended puts them in a potentially dangerous situation. If you must leave your room, open your door and alert someone, or pick up the telephone (if near by) and page for help.

SAFETY AND ACCIDENT PREVENTION

Young children remain in a high-risk category for accidents and require close supervision. They naturally have a curious nature and are interested in everything new they encounter. Curiosity often exceeds a child's life experiences. Children may really enjoy eating blue ice cream and may place blue window cleaner in the same category if they are thirsty. Medicine may be mistaken for candy their mom occasionally shares with them. Center staff must be aware of safety at all times when caring for young children. Purses should be

SUGGESTED FIRST AID DIRECTIVES

CHOKING

(Conscious) - Stand or kneel behind child with your arms around his waist and make a fist. Place thumb side of fist in the middle of abdomen just above the navel. With moderate pressure, use your other hand to press fist into child's abdomen with a quick, upward thrust. Keep your elbows out and away from child. Repeat thrusts until obstruction is cleared or child begins to cough or becomes unconscious.

(Unconscious) - Position child on his back. Just above navel, place heel of one hand on the midline of abdomen with the other hand placed on top of the first. Using moderate pressure, press into abdomen with a quick, upward thrust. Open airway by tilting head back and lifting chin. **If you can see the object**, do a finger sweep. Slide finger down inside of cheek to base of tongue, sweep object out but be careful not to push the object deeper into the throat. Repeat above until obstruction is removed or child begins coughing. If child does not resume breathing, proceed with artificial respiration (see below).

Infants - Support infant's head and neck. Turn infant face down on your forearm. Lower your forearm onto your thigh. Give four (4) back blows forcefully between infant's shoulder blades with heel of hand. Turn infant onto back. Place middle and index fingers on breastbone between nipple line and end of breastbone. Quickly compress breastbone one-half to one inch with each thrust. Repeat backblows and chest thrusts until object is coughed up, infant starts to cry, cough, and breathe, or medical personnel arrives and takes over.

POISONING

Call Poison Control Center (1-800-382-9097) immediately! Have the poison container handy for reference when talking to the center. Do not induce vomiting unless instructed to do so by a health professional. Check the child's airway, breathing, and circulation.

HEMORRHAGING

Use a protective barrier between you and the child (gloves). Then, with a clean pad, apply firm continuous pressure to the bleeding site for five minutes. Do not move/change pads, but you may place additional pads on top of the original one. If bleeding persists, call the doctor or ambulance Open wounds may require a tetanus shot.

SEIZURE

Clear the area around the child of hard or sharp objects. Loosen tight clothing around the neck. Do not restrain the child. Do not force fingers or objects into the child's mouth. After the seizure is over and if the child is not experiencing breathing difficulties, lay him/her on his/her side until he/she regains consciousness or until he/she can be seen by emergency medical personnel. After the seizure, allow the child to rest. Notify parents immediately. If child is experiencing breathing difficulty, or if seizure is lasting longer than 15 minutes, call an ambulance at once.

ARTIFICIAL RESPIRATION *(Rescue Breathing)*

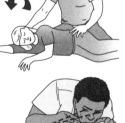

Position child on the back; if not breathing, open airway by gently tilting the head back and lifting chin. Look, listen, and feel for breathing. If still not breathing, keep head tilted back and pinch nose shut. Give two full breaths and then one regular breath every 4 seconds thereafter. Continue for one minute; then look, listen, and feel for the return of breathing. Continue rescue breathing until medical help arrives or breathing resumes.

If using one-way pulmonary resuscitation device, be sure your mouth and child's mouth are sealed around the device.

(Modification for infants only) Proceed as above, but place your mouth over nose and mouth of the infant. Give light puffs every 3 seconds.

SHOCK

If skin is cold and clammy, as well as face pale or child has nausea or vomiting, or shallow breathing, call for emergency help. Keep the child lying down. Elevate the feet. If there are head/chest injuries, raise the head and shoulders only.

FIGURE 6-1 Suggested First Aid Directives

Emergency Contacts: *Post Near Every Telephone*	

Your Facility Address: _____ *(Enter Street #/Apt. #)* _____

_____ *(Enter City)* _____

Nearest Main Intersection: _____ *(Enter Street #/Apt. #)* _____

Your Facility Phone Number: _____ *XXX-XXX-XXXX* _____

Contact	Phone Number
Operator	*XXX-XXX-XXXX*
Emergency	*XXX-XXX-XXXX*
Fire	*XXX-XXX-XXXX*
Police	*XXX-XXX-XXXX*
Consulting Dentist	*XXX-XXX-XXXX*
Poison Control	*XXX-XXX-XXXX*
Local Hospital Emergency Dept	*XXX-XXX-XXXX*
Other	

FIGURE 6–2 Emergency Contacts

stowed out of reach, preferably in a locked locker, cabinet, or closet. Cleaning fluids such as bleach solutions must be safely stowed at all times.

Food choices continue to require careful selection and preparation for three-year-old children, to avoid possible choking incidents. For best supervision, stick to a hard-and-fast rule that all food must be consumed at the table. Always calm the children before meals; begin with a song ending in whispers. The children are not yet skilled with modulating their voices independently and will not realize that the "group voice" has reached the level of a small roar. During mealtimes, seat a staff person at every table with the children as food is distributed family style. Concentrate on conversations, and gently encourage guidelines such as the use of "indoor voices," in order to listen carefully for choking. When the teacher communicates in a calm voice, discussing meaningful subjects, the children most often naturally mimic the same voice level and tone the adult is using.

Always ask, "What is the potential outcome of an action?" For example, "Can that large branch fallen from the tree become an eye-poking weapon in a curious child's hands?" And, finally, form the habit of performing quick safety checks of the room every morning before the children arrive. Scan for items inadvertently left behind by the evening cleaning crew or maintenance staff. This holds true for the playground as well. Continuously observe for trash, debris, poisonous weeds, or plants that could cause a safety hazard.

SAFETY PLUG COVERS

For the safety of all the children, check electrical outlets for safety plug covers on a daily basis. *It is important for safety plug covers to be in place at all times.* Young children are curious, and an unprotected electrical outlet is a potential for electrocution.

Standard 5.048, Safety Covers and Shock Protection Devices for Electrical Outlets, *Caring for Our Children National Health and Safety Performance Standards* (2nd ed., 2003), encourages the use of safety plug covers that are attached to the electrical receptacle by a screw or other means to prevent easy removal by a child. Avoid using outlet covers that a child can remove by extracting a plug from the socket. All newly installed electrical outlets accessible to children should be protected by GFCI (ground-fault circuit-interrupter) shock protection devices or safety receptacles that require simultaneous contact with both prongs of a plug to access the electricity. If you are planning new construction, consider placing the electrical outlets at least 48 inches from the ground. Several new safety plug outlets are now available for consumers. Form a regular habit of checking your electrical outlets for missing safety devices.

TOY SAFETY

Learning material safety is another important concern. Stuffed animals are best individually labeled and used by one child only during the resting period. Buy a "no-choke testing tube," available at better learning-material stores. If the object fits in the tube, then it is considered potentially dangerous to young children. Avoid using learning materials with long cords or strings, to avoid strangulation. Shorten cords or strings on push pull learning materials or clothing to no longer than 12 inches. Too many learning materials at once can be overwhelming and cause a tripping hazard. Limit the amount of learning materials on the floor at a given time. Select learning materials that do not present a strangulation hazard. Sharp edges and broken pieces on learning materials and on indoor and outdoor equipment are a potential danger—remove them immediately. Heed warning labels on learning materials. They are placed there by law in the United States. The Consumer Product Safety Commission (CPSC) has the authority to recall dangerous learning materials and products from the market. Also the mission of the State Public Interest Research Groups (PIRGs) is to help educate learning-material purchasers avoid the most common hazards in learning materials. For a complete list of learning-material tips and safety e-mail alerts, access World Against Toys Causing Harm, Inc. (W.A.T.C.H.) at http://www. toysafety.com.

SAFETY HELMETS

Preschool children are more confident than are toddlers with the use of their developing agility and are very attracted to riding learning materials, skates, and bicycles with training wheels. To prevent tragic head injuries, encourage the children to wear safety helmets bearing the Consumer Product Safety Commission (CPSC) seal of approval.

LATEX BALLOONS AND SMALL OBJECT HAZARDS

Latex balloons can be a very dangerous learning material for young children. Preschool children will attempt to inflate the balloons and run the risk of it deflating and blocking their airway. Best practices strongly discourage latex balloons, which should not be permitted in the child care facility where young children are in attendance. Mylar balloons are a safer choice. If the younger children share playground space with school-age children at different times of day, be very careful to clean up any latex pieces left by the older children. The same advice remains true for lending and swapping learning materials. Or, if an older class borrowed a set of the younger group's building blocks, to help construct their "block city," double-check the returned items for any errant small objects such as marbles or puzzle pieces that could present a hazard for the younger group.

INDIVIDUAL ACCIDENT REPORTS AND ACCIDENT-TRACKING REPORTS

If a child is injured during the course of the day complete an Accident/Incident Report (example in Figure 6–3). The accident report will describe the type of injury, its location on the body, and what time it occurred. Was blood present? If so, were universal precautions employed? What type of treatment was rendered, and who witnessed the accident? After this report is completed, send it to the director for review. The director or health professional will contact the family and inform them of the injuries so they can decide if they want further treatment for their child. It is a personal decision for the parents. Some are more likely to seek medical treatment than others, and it is a decision they are entitled to make. Some states require the center or teacher to submit a copy of the accident report to their licensing consultant if the injury required medical intervention with the doctor or clinic or hospital. This form is a legal document, so great care must be exercised to complete it accurately. Describe the injury rather than assign a diagnosis. An example of the nature of injury: "A purple mark the size of a dime on the right cheek" rather than "a bruise or contusion on the face." If you are unsure of how to describe the injury accurately, it is best to obtain assistance from a supervisor.

In centers, it is helpful to track trends with regards to illness or accidents. Create a binder specifically to collect and record all accident and illness reports. Log accidents and illnesses using the *Accident/Incident Tracking Reports*—see example in Figure 6–4. The director can use it as a handy reference to track possible illness trends such as influenza, Respiratory Synctial Virus (RSV) etc., or perhaps a pattern of accidents occurring in a specific group, such as biting or falls. This information is useful to plan potential areas for ongoing staff training. If your center maintains a copy of individual incident/accident reports or suggested illness reports discussed in the previous Chapter 5, "Health," it is advisable to store them in the binder with the illness and incident/accident tracking reports so they do not become part of the child's permanent record. Figure 6–5 is a flowchart and provides guidance for creating a file box or binder to store emergency and safety information. It is not uncommon for representatives from government agencies such as the Occupational Safety and Health Administration (OSHA) local fire marshals, firefighting personnel, or staff from program licensing agencies to visit and request to see this type of information.

FIELD TRIPS

Field trips outside of the center are a wonderful opportunity to extend learning experiences for the young preschool child. An excursion off the center premises, whether it is a trip to the zoo, or a neighborhood walk requires careful planning and attention to details to achieve a safe and successful journey.

Always choose personnel and volunteers who can fulfill roles necessary to promote safety. A leader such as the director, assistant director, or lead teacher, with current first aid and CPR training, should plan the excursion from beginning to end and execute the plan in person, so that a knowledgeable person is available to direct and solve any possible problems. A template for planning a well-organized and safe field trip is provided in the Field Trip Preparation Checklist located in the Forms and Templates Appendix. A field Trip Information Sheet is also provided in the Forms and Templates Appendix to help you keep attendance and actual information you will need to execute the plan, including the names and permission of all people attending that day. Always choose a qualified driver who is at least 21 years of age and has a valid driver's license for transporting passengers in a public

Accident/Incident

Child's name: _David (Enter Last Name)_____

Date of accident/injury: ___09/26/2005_____ Time: ___10:30 am_____

Brief description of accident/injury: _____David tripped over his_____

_____napping cot and bumped his right elbow causing small purple mark_____

_____about the size of a dime._____

Was first aid given? _____Yes_____ If so, describe: ____applied cold compress___

_____

Was blood present in accident? ___No___ How much? ____N/A_____

Were Universal Precautions employed? _____Not needed_____

Was medical intervention required?* ___No____ If yes, describe: _____

_____

Person initiating this report: ____Ms. Brown_____ Witness: _____Ben_____

Name of parent contacted: ___Mr. Allen_____ Time contacted: ___10:40 am___

Director's signature: ____Mrs. Neihoff_____

* In some states it is required to file a copy of this report with the child care licensing department if medical intervention is required.

Figure 6–3 Accident/Incident Report

Accident/Incident Tracking Reports

Name of Child	Date	Time Called	Type of Accident	Person Reporting Accident	Director Notified	Report Filed	Parent Notified	Time Called
David (Enter Last Name)	1/26	10:30 am	Fell & hurt right elbow	Ms. Runisfeld	✓	✓	✓	11:00 am
Agnes (Enter Last Name)	1/27	3:15 pm	Tripped & fell down, she scraped her left elbow & right knee	Mr. Meda	✓	✓	✓	3:30 pm

FIGURE 6–4 Accident/Incident Tracking Report

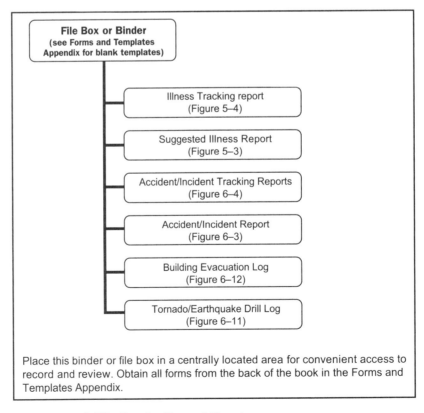

FIGURE 6–5 A File Box for Record Keeping

vehicle. Age, weight, and physical disabilities requiring wheelchairs are factors necessary to consider when arranging safe transport. Check with your local department of transportation for laws governing the use of safety restraint systems that are developmentally appropriate for children attending the field trip.

POSTING EMERGENCY EVACUATION PLANS AND EMERGENCY PHONE NUMBER LISTS

A list of emergency contacts for quick reference must be placed by every telephone in the center (see Figure 6–2 on p. 66). Conduct emergency fire and evacuation drills at least on a monthly basis. Every room where children are cared for requires a very specific outline of instructions and procedures that are to be followed in case of an emergency. Post this at each door, in each classroom, office, kitchen, etc. The instructions need to include what *exit* to be used in a situation requiring the children to be removed from the building (see Figure 6–6 for example). Create emergency evacuation ropes to use for the younger three-year-old children. Make ropes long enough for five to seven children. Tie a knot every 12 inches for the children to hold onto as staff guides them to a safe area. When the rope is not in use, place it on a hook out of reach, to avoid a potential strangulation accident. Use the ropes frequently to move from one place such as the indoor area to another such as the playground so the children become quite familiar with their usage. Once the children are able to form lines without difficulty, the ropes will no longer be necessary.

CONDUCTING EMERGENCY EVACUATION DRILLS

Familiarize yourself with the emergency evacuation procedures information long before a drill occurs. It is helpful to have a large blanket available and an emergency bag in case re-entry into the building is delayed (see Figure 6–7). Replenish and maintain the emergency bag at all times so it is available in a moments notice. Schedule drills to be conducted on a regular basis. Fire alarms are very loud and can be frightening for young children. Talk to them and prepare them for the drill ahead of time.

Call the children to quickly line up. Account for all children in attendance. If the door is cool, open it slowly; make sure fire or smoke isn't blocking your escape route. If your escape is blocked, close the door and use the alternative escape route. Smoke and heat rise. Be prepared to crawl where the air is clearer and cooler, near the floor. Move as far from the building as possible. Assemble the children and again account for all children in attendance. In case of a real fire do not re-enter the building until it is cleared by the proper authorities.

Emergency Evacuation Plan

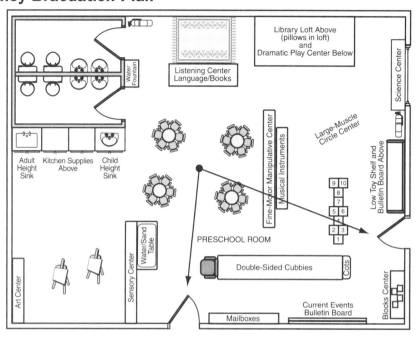

Draw first choice escape route; draw second choice escape route

Center's Address: _____ *(Enter Street #/Apt. #)* _____

Nearest Main Intersection: _____ *(Enter Street #/Apt. #)* _____

Center's Phone Number: _____ *XXX-XXX-XXXX* _____

In Case of Fire Call: _____ *XXX-XXX-XXXX* _____

In Case of Bomb Threat Call: _____ *XXX-XXX-XXXX* _____

In Case of Gas Leak Call: _____ *XXX-XXX-XXXX* _____

Fire Extinguisher Expires Date: _____ *11-05-2009* _____

Emergency Bag and Blanket Are Located: _____ *in closet of main hallway* _____

Stretch the evacuation rope out on the floor. Have each child grab a knot and hold tight. Account for all children in attendance. If the door is cool, open door slowly, make sure fire or smoke isn't blocking your escape route. If your escape is blocked, close the door and use alternative escape route. Smoke and heat rise. Be prepared to crawl where the air is clearer and cooler near the floor. Move as far from the building as possible. In case of a real fire, do not reenter the building until it is cleared by the proper authorities.

How to create an emergency evacuation rope:

Create an emergency evacuation rope by using a rope long enough for 5-7 children. Tie a knot every 12" for them to hold onto and guide them to a safe area.

When the rope is not in use, place it on a hook out of reach to avoid a potential strangulation accident.

    12"   **12"**   **12"**   **12"**   **12"**   **12"**   **12"**

FIGURE 6–6 Emergency Exit Evacuation

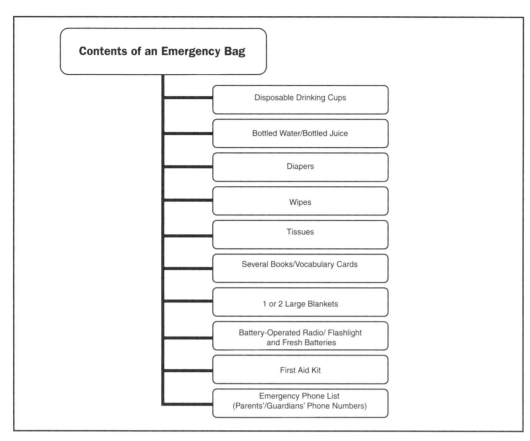

FIGURE 6–7 How to Assemble an Emergency Bag

RECORDING EMERGENCY EVACUATION DRILLS

Keep a record of what day and time the emergency drill takes place, and how long it takes for the center to completely evacuate all the children *safely* to their designated areas. Only one book is necessary to store emergency drill practices. Some centers assign one staff member to act as a safety captain. The safety captain works under the direction of the center director and not only oversees the drill schedule but also makes periodic inspections of learning materials, follows expiration dates on fire extinguisher and maintain accurate records of all drills conducted in the center. Evacuation drill examples are provided for Hurricane Emergency Instructions in Figure 6–8, Tornado Emergency Instructions in Figure 6–9, and Earthquake Emergency Instructions in Figure 6–10. Use them to customize a drill that is suitable for your specific circumstances. Blank templates are available in the Forms and Templates appendix. Figures 6–11 and 6–12 provide a Tornado/Earthquake Drill Log and Building Evacuation Log.

Hurricane Emergency Instructions

Hurricane/Tropical Storm Watch: indicates conditions are possible in the specified area within 36 hours.

Hurricane/Tropical Storm Warning: conditions are expected within 24 hours.

Send the children home.
Learn your specific evacuation route.
Secure your facility.
Close storm shutters.
Turn utilities off at main valves if instructed by authorities.
Take emergency phone numbers with you.

Your Evacuation Route: _____ *turn right on West 86th Street, drive 2 blocks to* _____

_____ *Meridian, turn right, go 1/2 a mile to Interstate 465 West for two miles, to Interstate 865 to* _____

_____ *Interstate 65 to North Carolina* _____

FIGURE 6–8 Hurricane Emergency Instructions

Tornado Emergency Instructions

Your county or region is: _____ *Marion County* _____

Tornado Watch: A tornado is possible. Remain alert for approaching storms. Tune your portable (battery-operated) radio to a local weather station.

Tornado Warning: A tornado has been sighted. Activate your emergency shelter plan immediately.

Grab your emergency bag and blanket. They are located: _____ *in main hallway* _____

_____

For two-year-olds – Stretch the evacuation rope out on the floor. Evacuation rope is located: _____ *in main hallway closet* _____
Have each child grab a knot and hold on tight. Account for all children in attendance.
Move children calmly and quickly to an interior room or hallway.
Your best location is: _____ *Main hallway past library* _____

_____

_____

_____

_____

_____

Cover the children with heavy blankets or cushions, if available, in case of flying glass or debris. Avoid windows, doors, outside walls, and corners of rooms.

FIGURE 6–9 Tornado Emergency Instructions

Earthquake Emergency Instructions

Prior to an earthquake:
- Brace high and top-heavy objects.
- Fasten cubbies, lockers, toy shelves to the wall.
- Anchor overhead lighting fixtures.
- Install flexible pipe fitting to avoid gas or water leaks.
- Know when and how to shut off electricity, gas, and water at main switches and valves.
- Locate safe spots in the room to protect yourself from dropping debris such as under a sturdy table or crib.

Your safest location is: _____ *in the hallway under library tables* _____

The shutoff for gas is located: _____ *in the basement next to furnace* _____

The water main is located: _____ *in the kitchen next to large sink* _____

Your emergency bag is located: _____ *top shelf of toy cabinet* _____

During an earthquake:

- Stay inside until shaking stops and it is safe to go outside.
- Move the children to your safe location (inside a crib on an inside wall).
- Describe where: _____ *Move children under the large library table located in hallway.* _____

_____

_____

_____

- Place a heavy blanket or lightweight mattress over the crib.
- If you are on the playground, move away from the building.

When the shaking stops be prepared for aftershocks. Check for injuries and administer first aid as indicated. Use flashlights if electricity is out. DO NOT light candles or matches in case of gas leakage.

FIGURE 6–10 Earthquake Emergency Instructions

Tornado / Earthquake Drill Log

Date	Time of Drill	Time Needed to Seek Cover	Comments	Full Name of Person In Charge
2/14	2:30 pm	2 minutes	Well Done!	Mrs. Ferdahard - Director

FIGURE 6–11 Tornado/Earthquake Drill Log

Building Evacuation Log

Date	Time of Drill	Evacuation Time	Comments	Full Name of Person in Charge
05-11	8:30 am	1 min, 50 sec	Great Job!	Mrs. Ferrie Director
06-24	2:45 pm	2 min, 10 sec	Review plan with new assistant	Mrs. Ferrie Director
07-08	3:45 pm	2 min, 5 sec	Improved	Mrs. Ferrie Director

FIGURE 6–12 Building Evacuation Log

REFERENCES

American Academy of Pediatrics, American Public Health Association, National Resource Center for Health and Safety in Child Care. *Stepping stones to using caring for our children,* 2nd ed. (2003). p. 74.

Indiana State Board of Health. (2002). *Health care program for child care centers suggested first aid directives.* Information Sheet. Retrieved December 21, 2004, from http://www.in.gov.

To find your specific
State's Licensing, Rules
and Regulations go to:

http://nrc.uchsc.edu

Facilitating Three-Year-Olds and Their Families

CHAPTER 7

SPREAD THE WORD: ARRIVAL

Everyone appreciates a warm hello and welcome on arrival. Make an effort to greet your children and their families as they arrive. Many three-year-olds are becoming more comfortable in a social setting, especially if they have already experienced out-of-home care arrangements. Once they feel at home in the child care setting, they are usually quite happy to arrive at school. Their relationship with peers takes on a new importance. If this is their first experience away from their family, they may initially experience a period of separation anxiety when they first join the group. During this phase it is sometimes difficult for the young preschool child to part with a family member without tears.

Another factor to note is every parent and child has their own style for sharing a good-bye. Some parents will appreciate if you take their child so they can leave, and others will spend time with their child hanging up belongings, helping them become situated at the breakfast table, or selecting a learning material the child will enjoy. It is important to determine with the parents how you can best assist with the morning arrival and a smooth separation.

Collecting pertinent information during morning arrival allows the teachers to provide continuous care for each child. Because morning arrivals are a very busy time for the teachers, it is important to establish a means for families to communicate pertinent information to the staff that is relevant for each child's care that day. Avoid losing, missing, or forgetting communications. Spread the Word is a document that will provide a method to gather written communication between the families and the staff. Encourage the families to use this form to communicate requests such as *"Kyle has a doctor's appointment at 3:00 p.m., please change him into his clean outfit,"* or *"Caroline went to bed late last night (her grandparents are in town) so she is very tired and cranky this morning,"* or *"I will not be in the office today; I can be reached at the American Meeting Hall; my cell phone number is XXX-XXXX."* An example of Spread the Word can be seen in Figure 7–1. Copy the Spread the Word template in the Forms and Templates Appendix to gather pertinent specific information from the parent. Place the Spread the Word sheet on a clipboard, near other communication documents, such as the Medication Sheet. Be certain to understand the policies your center might observe with regard to written communication between families and the staff. If confidentiality is a concern, provide individual sheets of papers and envelopes for the parents to seal and drop in a basket or box specifically designated to collect the information. Place information-gathering documents in an area easily accessible to the families for recording information on arrival. Parents often work in offices where outdated envelopes are plentiful. Recycled envelopes serve a useful purpose for in-house use such as these in the center.

Spread The Word:
Check with your director on where to place this.
Some centers prefer a closed notebook approach.

Spread The Word

Date: _June 6th_

Harrison started a new antibiotic yesterday. His Dr.
advises us to watch for possible side effects such as a rash
or itching. Please call me if you notice any changes.

Mrs. Carol

Kara's grandmother (Mrs. Williams) will pick her up
after nap today, they are going to the Children's Museum.

Mr. Tom

Pedro is missing his little blue "nappy." Please help us
locate it today.

Mrs. Maria

Faizaan is very excited to attend the zoo field trip.
Do you need more volunteeers?

Mrs. C.

Center staff, please initial after reading: _AW_ _RAB_ _MP_ _DG_ _NS_

FIGURE 7–1 Spread The Word Example

CREATE A DAILY OUTLINE

Creating a Daily Outline was discussed previously in the text. In review, the Daily Outline is a brief summary of the group's planned daily schedule. An example of a completed Daily Outline was reviewed in Chapter 3 and is shown in Figure 3–3. It is designed in a simple format to provide a quick orientation for a substitute teacher and for parents seeking future care who are steady visitors at the center. The information found on the Simple Outline will give them a general idea what a common day in the group looks like. The daily outline lists the planned day of activities with the corresponding times noted but does not offer any specific details. Specific details are outlined next in the Daily Schedule Details. A blank template for creating your own daily outline is located in the Forms and Templates Appendix. The daily outline schedule provides a method for the substitute teachers and other program personnel to quickly orient themselves to your group before diving immediately into the details.

The Forms and Templates Appendix provides a template for reproducing and creating your own Daily Outline classroom schedule. Fill in the blanks to reflect the typical schedule you have developed for the preschool children you care for. Maintain this schedule so it is always a current version of the children's planned day. Typically the Daily Outline is updated at least every season, especially in climates that warrant a modification in types of play activities due to changing weather.

CREATE A DETAILED CLASSROOM SCHEDULE

The Daily Schedule Details is a more indepth look at the day, providing information about where to find things, why we do this, and who has specific instructions for care. To observe the example of the Three-Year-Old Classroom Schedule Details, discussed previously in Chapter 3, "Establishing an Excellent Path for Communication," refer back to Figure 3–4. Detailed descriptions of the daily activities are outlined here as well as specific information including relevant information such as noting allergies children might have or early arrival time for a child on a particular day necessitating his eating breakfast. ("Connor and Ariel eat breakfast every day," or "Tamika has a milk allergy.") Paint a picture with words describing the children's whole day. The information provided *in detail* will promote consistent and *safe* care, in your absence. The children will experience the familiar routines you have established and will certainly provide the substitute teacher with the confidence needed to fulfill his or her tasks. A Classroom Schedule Details blank template can be found in the Forms and Templates Appendix. Duplicate the template, and fill in the blanks accordingly. Update this schedule at least quarterly or with each season change, to accurately reflect the detailed schedule you have planned for your group of preschool children.

LESSON PLANS

Once the Classroom Schedule Details form is completed, the weekly lesson plan is the next endeavor. Lesson plans are your blueprint for each day. Lesson planning is a crucial element for achieving an enriched environment and a satisfying experience for the children's care. An example of a lesson plan is provided in this chapter (see Figure 7–2). A blank Lesson Plan template is located in the Forms and Templates Appendix. Use this template to create lesson plans for the preschool group. Many creative and comprehensive books are available to assist with lesson-planning ideas: Check the Recommended Resources list.

Threes Weekly Lesson Plans

Stage of Play Development: Emerging from parallel play into symbolic and early stages of cooperative play

Group Name: *"The Sunflowers" Preschool*

Theme: *Nighttime*   **Lead Teacher:** *Ms. Laura*

Week of: *Jan 3–9*

Activities	Sun	Mon	Tues	Wed	Thurs	Fri	Sat
Concept		Owls	Little and Big	Sleeping	Moon	Get in line	
Circle Time (Whole Group)		What day is it?	What should I wear for the weather?	Hello to everyone.	Today's song is?	What am I doing today?	
Language Skills							
KIDEX Fun with Language & Telling Tales Activities		Owls books	Size books	Sleeping books	Frank Asch moon books	Finger play Follow the leader	
Songs/Finger Plays		Crayon Hoot?	"I'm a Little Teapot"	Finger play: No more monkeys jumping on the bed	Poem: "Twinkle Twinkle Little Star"	Discussion Why do I have to get in line?	
Reading/Stories (Flannel Board/ Vocabulary/ Puppets)		Story: Good-Night Owl, Pat Hutchins	Story: Big Ones, Little Ones, Tana Hoban	When Cats Dream, Dav Pilkey	Story: Goodnight Moon Margaret Wise Brown	Story: There's no such thing as a dragon, Jack Kent	
KIDEX: *Exploring Our World* Activities		Owl eyes	Measure big blocks and small blocks	Record children snoring sounds	No light – no color	Drawing lines in sand	
Cognitive/Sensory/Math/ Science Centers		Owl matching	M&M size sorting	Quilt square counting	Cooking Moon rock recipe	Front, middle, back of line positions	
KIDEX: *Creating My Way* Activities Arts Exploration/ Crafts		Feather painting	Big & little brush painting	Toothbrush painting	Chalk art (black paper, white chalk)	Ruler art Straight line	
Dramatic Play Center		Stuffed owl play	Mommies - Daddies - Babies	Pajama play	Trip to the moon	Ticket booth	
KIDEX: *My Body Is Wonderful* Activities — Large Muscle & Music Movement		Fly like a bird (swooping and soaring)	Big Steps & Little Steps	Slipper races Pillow jump	Flashlight tag Rocket to the moon	Follow the leader Mama duck and ducklings Dragon parade Choo-choo train	
Small Muscle Movement		Buttons, snaps	Big Puzzles Little Puzzles	Blanket folding Tuck me in	Moon rock Foil & paper crumbling	Beads and strings	

Learning Centers

Housekeeping / Dramatic Play / Sensory
Science / Fine Motor / Art / Water & Sand Table
Math / Active Play / Music Movement / Toys
Library / Music / Listening / Blocks / Computer

Self-Help Skills / Social Skills

37–48 Months—Integrate and encourage the development of skills during this 12-month span

- Follows directions most of the time
- Helps with clean up
- Verbal skills building
- Basic manners (please & thank you)
- Respects others, space & property
- Basic self-control skills
- Shares most of the time

- Feeds self independently
- Proper hygiene (toilet flushing, hand washing, tooth brushing)
- Manages own clothing (except small buttons)

- Refining body movements
- Body / Self awareness
- Safety awareness
- Building imagination
- Converses with peers
- Follows class rules
- Cooperates with peers

FIGURE 7–2 Weekly Lesson Plan Example

Keep a copy of your current lesson plan in this section of the KIDEX Class Book for your handy reference and all staff members that care for the children. Post the lesson plan somewhere visible, such as the Current Events Bulletin Board, for future and current families to review. Place a copy in the KIDEX Class Book for teachers and substitutes to refer to.

MEETING IN THE CIRCLE

By the time children reach a preschool age they are ready to begin sharing social experiences derived by meeting in planned circle-time activities. Circle time teaches children how to interact in a group and develop critical thinking skills, by the act of sharing and listening to their teachers and peers, they gain personal confidence. Actually the possibilities for learning and growing are just about infinite. Many teachers find a large-group meeting to be a great way to begin the day; it is an opportunity to share the day's schedule, discuss plans, and touch base with the children.

The length of time planned for the group will depend on the ages of the preschool children. Younger three-year-olds have a less developed attention span and can only sit for about 10 to 15 minutes. Use activities such as jumping, running, or dancing in place to break up the "sit time" as a way to get enough time to finish the session. Don't create a group too large to manage smoothly, and do allow adequate time to interact with the children at a suitable pace. Develop a variety of techniques to gain the children's attention by inviting them to participate through singing, books, stories, finger plays, or hands-on activities. Develop a ritual such as a song or motion to signal the beginning and ending of circle time. Planning interesting and meaningful circle time meetings can fuel already budding imaginations and provide pleasures the young children will eagerly anticipate when the circle is called.

Circle time is a perfect place to explore similarities and differences among the children in the group. Many rich opportunities can be shared about families and how they live. Adoptive parents, single parents, two parents, children reared by grandparents, and multiracial families are just some of the many areas that can be introduced in a casual setting of circle time. Spotlighting a new child every couple of weeks allows time to work with the child's family to provide photos, traditional games they play, and foods they enjoy—just to name a few ideas. Offering all the children an opportunity to gain an insight to how other families live and what constitutes a family unit fosters early acceptance of others' likes and differences.

TRACKING MILESTONES OF DEVELOPMENT AND EVALUATING PROGRESS

Best practices encourage early care and education programs to maintain current records on children's growth and developmental patterns. The following will provide a guide for observing and recording development of milestones for each preschool child. Figures 7–3 and 7–4 group developmental activities typically observed around age 3 to 3½ years (37–42 months) and activities typically observed around 3½ to 4 years (43–48 months). *It is very important to understand from the beginning that all children are individuals. Every child will develop at similar rates but at a pattern unique to that child.* They each have their own unique personalities, so consequently they will develop at a slightly different pace. The checklist provided is a broad viewpoint suggesting approximate developmental milestones that can be expected for a child 3 to 3½ years old. If you find a child is not showing most of the characteristics listed, there can be many reasons. Remember

3 - 3 1/2 Years

37 – 42 Months

DEVELOPMENTAL MILESTONES

THREES CAN:

___Y___ SPEAK IN 4 – 6 WORD SENTENCES

___Y___ FOLLOW SIMPLE DIRECTIONS MOST OF THE TIME

___Y___ NAME BASIC COLORS (RED, BLUE, GREEN, ORANGE)

___Y___ SORT OBJECTS INTO TWO CATEGORIES (BIG/SMALL, RED/BLUE)

___Y___ COMPLETE: 6 – 7 PIECE PUZZLES

___N___ BEGIN TO PARTICIPATE IN GROUP ACTIVITIES

___N___ WALK FORWARD AND BACKWARD ON A LINE

___Y___ RIDE A TRICYCLE

___N___ MAKE A BALL OUT OF CLAY

___Y___ UNDERSTAND SIMPLE GAMES

___Y___ ROLL A LARGE BALL AT A TARGET

___Y___ CLIMB UP AND DOWN STAIRS UNASSISTED

___N___ STRING LARGE BEADS (4-5 BEADS)

___S___ DRESS AND UNDRESS INDEPENDENTLY (NEEDS HELP WITH SMALL BUTTONS OR LACES)

___Y___ ZIP AND UNZIP

___S___ WASH AND DRY HANDS INDEPENDENTLY

___Y___ STACK 5 – 10 BLOCKS

___N___ NAME BASIC BODY PARTS

___Y___ PAINT WITH A LARGE BRUSH

___Y___ USE PLEASE AND THANK YOU

___S___ HELP WITH CLEAN UP

___S___ USE TOILET INDEPENDENTLY

___N___ WILLING TO SHARE SOMETIMES

___Y___ PAIR OBJECTS THAT ARE RELATED

> *Important Note: children will develop at similar rates but each in a unique pattern. If you find a child is not exhibiting the majority of characteristics listed, there could be many plausible reasons ranging from premature birth to a more reserved and cautious personality. This list is a broad overview and not inclusive of all developmental milestones three-year-olds experience.*

Y = YES	S = SOMETIMES	N = NOT YET

Child's Name: _____Julio (Enter Last Name)_____ Teacher: _____Ms. Dana_____

Date Initiated: _____6/2_____ Date Completed: _____7/5_____

FIGURE 7–3 37–42 Months Developmental Milestones

3 1/2 - 4 Years

43 – 48 Months
DEVELOPMENTAL MILESTONES

THREES CAN:

___Y___ USE PRONOUNS CORRECTLY (HE, SHE, IT, HER)

___Y___ BEGIN TO UNDERSTAND TIME CONCEPTS (DAY/NIGHT)

___Y___ CATCH A LARGE BALL

___Y___ USE FINGER WITH CONTROL TO PAINT OR PASTE

___Y___ BEGIN CUTTING IN A LINE

___N___ NAME BASIC SHAPES (CIRCLE, SQUARE, TRIANGLE)

___Y___ COUNT 3 – 5 OBJECTS

___Y___ KICK A BALL IN MOTION

___Y___ HOLD CRAYON WITH FINGERS NOT FIST

___S___ LISTEN TO SHORT STORIES OR BOOKS (7 – 9 MINUTES)

___Y___ THROW A BALL OVERHAND ACCURATELY

___N___ LACE STRING IN SHOES OR A SEQUENCE OF HOLES

___Y___ UNDERSTAND OPPOSITES (HOT/COLD, ON/OFF)

___Y___ ACT OUT SIMPLE STORIES

___S___ DRAW LINES (HORIZONTAL, VERTICAL)

___Y___ UNDERSTAND THAT PEOPLE ARE ALIKE AND DIFFERENT

___N___ POUR LIQUID FROM ONE CONTAINER TO ANOTHER

___Y___ SCREW AND UNSCREW LIDS, TOYS, ETC.

___N___ USE ADJECTIVES TO DESCRIBE

___S___ MEMORIZE AND RECITE SHORT NURSERY RHYMES OR SONGS

___Y___ ENGAGE IN IMAGINATIVE PLAY

___N___ SHOW CONCERN FOR PEERS

___Y___ PLAY WITH OTHER CHILDREN COOPERATIVELY

> *Important Note: children will develop at similar rates but each in a unique pattern. If you find a child is not exhibiting the majority of characteristics listed, there could be many plausible reasons ranging from premature birth to a more reserved and cautious personality. This list is a broad overview and not inclusive of all developmental milestones three-year-olds experience.*

Y = YES	S = SOMETIMES	N = NOT YET

Child's Name: ___Bjorn (Enter Last Name)___   Teacher: ___Mr. Don___

Date Initiated: ___6/2___   Date Completed: ___7/5___

FIGURE 7–4 43–48 Months Developmental Milestones

that children may "cross" stages of development according to their particular growth pattern. For example, the child who is using more energy in physical growth may not be as advanced in language development. Learning is not an even process. A child who is reserved may avoid certain activities over others but not necessarily to his or her detriment. If a child consistently does not exhibit signs of achieving most of the outlined milestones, with a consistent lag behind others, then perhaps more exploration is in order. It is advisable to share your concerns with the director or program supervisor for consideration.

Review the milestones of development on a regular basis at least every five to six weeks. Note areas in which the child is still learning and areas where the child has mastered certain skills.

1. Check the behaviors with a (*Y*) for "yes" if the child demonstrates this action regularly.
2. Mark (*S*) for "sometimes" if the child is still practicing and only demonstrates this action sometimes.
3. Mark (*N*) for "not yet" if the child doesn't demonstrate this action yet. Use the listed developments as a guide for observing.

Place the Milestones of Development that are in progress on an individual clipboard for each child with the Activities and Play Opportunities sheet, or store them in the KIDEX Class Book.

PLANNING ACTIVITIES AND PLAY OPPORTUNITIES

Young children are growing, learning, and developing in so many ways one cannot expect them to become an expert at everything. Because each child develops at their own individual pace, familiarize yourself with activities that are appropriate for each stage of development. Figures 7–5 and 7–6 provide a variety of planned activities that assist with building large- and small-muscle control, language skills, sensory responses, science, math, mental cognition, and social growth. The activities and play opportunities templates provide a variety for play in all the aforementioned areas. Choose activities from five sections: *My Body Is Wonderful, Creating My Way, Exploring My World, Fun with Language,* and *Telling Tales.* For maximum practice, choose one activity from each of the five sections when planning activities on the lesson plan for the children. This will provide plenty of variety. How long each activity lasts will depend solely on the child's level of interest. Feel free to repeat activities. Young children are comforted by repetition and enjoy the feeling of success in practicing their new skills. If your center already has a planned curriculum, then use the *KIDEX Activities and Play Opportunities* as a supplement for early morning, late afternoon, and evening activities or to enrich with a broad variety of choices.

MY BODY IS WONDERFUL

Once children reach the preschool years, their bodies will become more agile and coordinated. The children are relating physically to their environment and learning words such as *over, under,* and *around.* The children continue to learn a sense of identity by exploring with their bodies and learning about their own unique physical capabilities. Large-muscle and small-muscle activities provide practice for refining their rapidly developing mobility. Young three-year-olds are more capable than they were just 6 months ago but they continue to benefit from close supervision. They still do not have enough information to avoid dangerous situations. Or, as their imagination grows they simply may forget the "bad guys"

3 - 3 1/2 Years Activities

Telling Tales — Simple Picture Books — Language Activities

Category	
1	• Create color books. Before beginning the project, have several pictures of different colored items cut out for the children to sort. Have a color word on paper and allow the children to paste pictures to the correct paper. Put the pages together to create the book.
	• Share simple picture books with the children that show different body parts. Have the children point to his/her own body parts as you read the story. (e.g., *Can you find your knee?*)
	• Read a variety of simple Dr. Seuss books. The children will enjoy the rhythm and rhyme of the books. *In a People House* can give them a chance to name objects and find them around the room. Other books allow the children opportunities to "fill in" rhyming words.
	• Create a "How to" book on washing hands. Discuss and practice washing hands the correct way, then have the children help write a book about it. You can take pictures of the children at each step to help illustrate it. You could do this with many multi-step procedures you may have in your room.
	• Provide books that only have pictures and encourage the children to create their own story about the characters. Have some stories the children know and don't know, so they can recall stories or create their own stories.
	• Read favorite books over and over again to familiarize the children with the language and characters.
	• Read familiar stories, like *Goldilocks and the Three Bears* or *The Gingerbread Man*, and let the children use a felt board and felt characters to act out the stories.
	• Make a book of fabric for the children. Be sure to include a variety of fabrics with different colors and textures. Ask them to describe the fabrics.
	• Read familiar books and change words to silly words and allow them to correct you. When rereading a *Clifford: The Big Red Dog* book, call the dog "Georgie" or some other name.
	• Share stories that are about sharing and playing with other children.
	• Create books that go along with your theme. If your theme is the snow, have the children cut out pictures of things that you can do in the snow. Have them paste the pictures on paper. You write "I can _____." on each page, filling in the blank with what is being done in the picture (e.g., sled, ice skate, ski, make a snow angel, etc.).
	• Provide a variety of books that the children can connect with. If you live near the ocean, provide books about the ocean and ocean animals for the children to look at. If you live in a busy city, then make sure you have books with pictures of your own city or any big city.
	• Read books that have nursery rhymes or songs. If the children know the rhyme or song, then they can read with you.
	• Read *The Very Hungry Caterpillar* and create a book about the very hungry children in your room. Have them each draw or cut and paste a picture of their favorite food. Put the pages together and add a hole or "bite" in each page.

FIGURE 7–5 37–42 Months Activities

Activities 3 – 3½ Years Continued

Fun With Language Activities

- Sing, sing, and sing! Teach the children simple songs or rhymes that you can sing over and over again. You may want to sing a morning song to start the day and a good-bye song to end the day.
- Share pictures of different people or faces and have the children describe how they feel, what they are wearing, what they are doing, etc.
- Provide opportunities to learn opposites. Have different kinds of food available to try and describe (e.g., The soup is hot; the juice is cold. Carrots are hard; marshmallows are soft.). Also demonstrate opposites or have the children "find" opposites. (The cup is full/empty. The lights are on/off.)
- Plan experiences for the children to participate in and then discuss. Recall what they saw, did, ate, etc. Go on field trips, walks outside, or little indoor adventures.
- Encourage them to use their imagination as well. Share or create stories about imaginary experiences. Pretend you are searching for whales in your imaginary boat or submarine.
- Discuss favorite stories and characters. Describe them together.
- Be positive about pronunciation errors. Encourage them to continue thinking and to try new words and ways to say something.
- Play copycat games where the children imitate letter sounds or silly sounds that you make.
- Ask questions about their day. Did you like playing outside? What was your favorite thing you did outside?
- If you are given short or one-word answers, ask more open-ended questions to encourage more communication.
- Show pictures of two related items and ask what the differences and similarities are between the two (e.g., hold up a picture of a green motorcycle and a green truck).
- Go on a hunt of the unknown. Have a child find something outside, in the room, or somewhere else that they don't know what it is called. Describe it together and tell the child what it is called.
- Ask questions about things they have done before or places they have gone before. Try to help them recall as much information as they can.
- Place a favorite toy or object around the room. Encourage the children to tell you where it is located (e.g., The truck is under the table. The truck is next to or beside the chair.).
- Sing the ABC song to get them acquainted with the letters.

Category
2

FIGURE 7–5 37–42 Months Activities

Activities 3 – 3½ Years Continued

My Body Is Wonderful — Large & Small Muscle Activities

- Provide a variety of riding toys for the children to use in a large area. Create a track or obstacle course for the children to steer through. Have children role play police officers, parking attendants, etc.
- Read stories or discuss different animals, then have the children use clay or play dough to mold the characters and then recreate the story.
- Play simple follow the leader games and let the children lead at times. Encourage jumping, skipping, hopping, rolling, etc.
- Set up small carnival-like games that give each child opportunities to throw a bean bag or ball at a target, roll the ball to knock down the pins, etc.
- Have the children work on fine motor skills in centers, such as stringing large beads, zipping, buttoning, snapping, lacing shoes, etc.

Category	
3	- Lead the children in different motions to songs. You can jump to the music, clap, stomp, or do any other large movements. Make up motions to songs and teach the children (e.g., touch your toes, pinch your nose, etc.).
	- Give children streamers or ribbons to hold onto and have them dance to music.
	- Provide a small wagon for outdoor play. Bring balls or outside toys and have them move the items from one place to another. They must fill up the wagon and carefully roll it to a new place and unload it.
	- Use a metal cookie sheet and magnets. Allow the children to move the magnets around. You can cut out different body parts (head, body, legs, arms, feet, hands), stick them to a magnetic table and have the children "build" a body.
	- Fill a large container with small items, such as keys, large bolts, and large marbles. Have the children sort the items into smaller containers
	- Lead the children in simple exercises (touch your toes, reach for the sky, jump up and down, etc.). This is a good way to start the day and get those muscles working.
	- When walking outside or to another room, have them tip toe like mice or walk sideways.
	- Make a cutting pool. Place all sorts of materials that children can cut (varieties of paper, yarn, etc.) in a small wading pool. Have a bucket of scissors in the pool. Invite the children to cut in the pool. The cut materials can be used in future crafts.
	- Line up several small hula-hoops and have the children jump from hoop to hoop.
	- Provide a small teeter-totter on the playground. Show the children how to use it, and then let them push themselves up and down.

FIGURE 7–5 37–42 Months Activities

Activities 3 – 3½ Years Continued

Creating My Way — Creative Exploration

- Create simple cut and paste activities for the children to complete. Provide scissors to cut out pictures of things that make the child happy and paste them to the big smiley face page. Cut out different size circles and paste them together the world's silliest snowman.

- Marble painting. Drop marbles in paint, place a piece of paper in a box with a lid, spoon the paint-covered marbles in the box, put the lid on tightly, and let the child shake it up. (You may want to tape the lid down just in case.)

- Fill various cups with colored water. Place the cups of water in the water table and allow them to explore pouring the water on paper, mixing the colors, etc. Add soap to make it a little more fun with bubbles.

- Provide large paper and large paintbrushes for the children to paint pictures. Make sure the paint is washable and the children wear smocks. It can get messy!

- To help children gain more fine motor control, provide coloring pages of shapes and non-detailed pictures of animals for them to practice "coloring in the lines." Because creativity is limited by this activity, encourage them to use their imagination (e.g., purple dogs, orange grass, etc.).

- Paint with nature. Collect leaves, twigs, flowers, and other items to paint or print with.

- Have them practice tracing straight, curvy, and zigzag lines.

- Let them paint objects other than paper, such as pieces of wood, rocks, sticks, etc.

- Make a picture frame and let the children decorate it. You can make a square out of tongue depressors or cut a frame out of cardboard. Once the frame is made, let the children paste shells, feathers, buttons, etc. onto the frames.

- Let them paint with their feet. This is an outdoor activity and make sure they have shorts on or their pants are rolled up. Put washable paint in a shallow tray and have one child at a time step in the paint. Make sure a long sheet of butcher paper is right next to the tray and have them walk, hop, or tip toe on the paper. Be sure to have a bucket of water to wash their feet off nearby.

Category

4

- Finger paint with the primary colors (red, yellow, blue). Give them two colors at a time so they can discover what happens when they mix the colors.

- Add flour or corn starch to paint so they can make bumpy paintings.

- Make wet chalk drawings. Give them dark construction paper, chalk, and a small cup of water. Have them dip the chalk into the water and then draw on the paper.

- Create paper plate masks. Allow them to decorate a paper plate with different materials. You will need to cut the eyeholes for them and glue a tongue depressor to the bottom of the plate. Then they have a mask on a stick.

- Have the children try to tear different shapes out of paper. Paste the shapes on paper to create a torn shape collage.

FIGURE 7-5 37–42 Months Activities

Activities 3 – 3½ Years Continued

	Exploring Our World — Activities to Explore Cognitive, Pre-Math, Sensory, and Science
	• Create a small garden space for the group. Have the children dig holes and plant seeds that they can tend to and watch grow. If there is no space for a garden, you can grow seeds in cups or plastic bags (place a folded, wet paper towel and a lima bean seed in a bag and watch the seed grow).
	• Go on a nature hunt to find different shapes and textures. It can be made into a scavenger hunt as well (e.g., find something smaller than your hand, find a green leaf, find something round).
	• Have the children help you count the class when you line up to go outside, count objects you get out, etc.
	• Have the children sort pictures of people doing activities into different categories, such as things you do at night and things you do in the day.
Category 5	• Provide the children with blocks and toy cars. Encourage them to build roads or a city to "drive" the cars around on.
	• Make popsicles. Have the children help make fruit juice and pour it into small cups. Set a popsicle stick in the cup, so you have something to hold on to. You can keep checking on the popsicles to see how long it takes them to freeze. Then enjoy!
	• Provide manipulatives for the children to explore and sort, such as beans, small jars, beads, etc.
	• Use masking tape on the floor to create large shapes. Have the children walk along to tape that forms the shapes. Ask the name of the shape before a child walks it.
	• Make a bubble solution, then blow the bubbles and watch the wind blow the bubbles around.
	• Talk about the weather. Is it cloudy, rainy, or sunny?
	• Let children play with the lights out (make sure there is a little light so they are not scared). Give each child a flashlight and allow them to experiment with shadows.
	• Go on a color hunt around the room or outside.
	• Challenge them to stack small cube blocks as high as they can.
	• Mix colored water and oil, pour it in a clear plastic bottle, seal it tightly, and then let the children shake it up and see what happens. Add small beads or sequins to make it more exciting.
	• Make sun prints. Go on a hunt for small items in nature, such as twigs, flowers, leaves, and rocks. On a sunny day place these nature items of sheets of construction paper. Leave it sitting where it won't be disturbed. If you take the items off several hours later, there will be a print where the items were placed on the paper.

FIGURE 7–5 37–42 Months Activities

3 1/2 - 4 Years Activities

Category	
1	**Telling Tales — Simple Picture Books – Language Activities**

* Go on a treasure hunt for rhyming words. You will need to lead them to words, such as *look at Sammie's pretty hair, hmm...let's see if we can find something in the room that sounds like hair. There is the wall, a table, a chair...*The children will figure the rhyming words out and as you find objects that rhyme, take a Polaroid or digital picture. Label each picture and put them together to form a book of rhyming words.

* Create a book of class creations. It could be a collection of photos of block creations or any artistic creations they made in class. Label the pictures and bind them together to form a book. Or you could put pages that the children colored together to make a book of artwork.

* Provide books about people in the community, jobs, etc. that will foster dramatic play (e.g., if you read a book about a doctor visit, then you can turn the dramatic play area into a hospital.)

* Make finger puppets or regular puppets and have the children act out the stories as you read or recreate the stories later.

* Create a simple repeated line book, such as *The bear is blue. The bear is yellow.* Pointing to the words as you read helps the children see a connection between the text and the picture — the letters say something, they have a meaning.

* When getting ready to read a book, hold the book the wrong way. Say, "I'm ready to read this book." Let the children correct you and tell you how you are supposed to hold the book.

* Read *Something is Going to Happen* by Charlotte Zolotow. Give each child a picture of a front door open on a house. Have the children draw what they wish to see outside their front door. Put these pages together to make a class book.

* Find books that have at least two characters in the pictures. Have the students become the "sound track" of the book. Have them share what they think the characters are saying to each other.

* When reading a book, create voices for the different characters. The children will love to try and imitate your voice.

* Throughout the year let the children draw pictures of whatever they want and then have them tell you what it is a picture of. Write what they say at the bottom of the page. Save several of these pieces, and then put them together to make an art book that the child can share with her parents at the end of the year.

* Have the children create a book of who lives in their home. Give them a page shaped like a house for each member of their family (don't forget pets!) and have them draw each person or animal. Write their names (e.g.,mom, dad, Sam, Lana, and Goldie) on the pages for the child.

* Read books that require responses from the children, such as a train noise or a dog bark. This will keep them involved. They have to be good listeners so they don't miss the chance to make the noise.

* Share a variety of books about one subject and have them compare the stories and characters (e.g., if you are talking about kangaroos, you can read *Kangaroo* by Caroline Arnold, *Noel the Coward* by Robert Kraus, and *Katy-No-Pocket* by Emmy Payne).

* Find books that will help the children kick bad habits (e.g., thumb sucking) or teach them good habits (e.g., covering your mouth when you sneeze).

* Share books with numbers in them, so the children can begin to recognize numerals.

FIGURE 7–6 43–48 Months Activities

Activities 3½ - 4 Years Continued

Fun With Language Activities

- Take a short book with a simple plot apart and laminate the pages (or you can make your own short story). Have the children put the pages in the correct sequence.
- Model conversation and encourage the children to have conversations together.
- Start to introduce sounds that are made at the beginning of words. *Popcorn starts with the "p" sound, what else starts with that sound?* Hunt around the room or outside for ideas.
- Encourage the children to use "please" and "thank you" throughout the day. Be sure to set an example.
- They love to ask who, what, when, and where questions at this age. Answer the questions or explore together to find the answers.
- Teach them short tongue twisters. They love to try and say the silly sentences (e.g., Susie sells seashells at the seashore).
- Play "I Spy" a little differently by giving clues about an object or person. Use descriptive words and talk about words you use that they may not know.

Category

2

- Discuss what happened today, earlier today, or yesterday; model the appropriate language to use when you describe something that already happened.
- Sing songs that give directions. Think of what you want them to do and you can sing it to any tune that you know. If it is something you will say over and over again, try to keep it the same (e.g., sing "Put your coat away and sit in a circle" in the same tune every time you come inside from playing).
- Teach them how to use soft voices, medium (inside) voices, and loud (outside) voices. Discuss when you would use each one.
- Each day, draw a mystery word from a box. Each time the children hear the word have them show silent applause (raise hands straight up in the air and wiggle your fingers). This is a listening activity that lasts the whole day. You can also introduce new words.
- Encourage parents to ask their child about her day. They can even write it down in a journal and read it back to the child occasionally. It is a fun way to keep parents involved and informed.
- Use a box to teach placement and opposite words (e.g., top/bottom, inside/outside, front/back, etc.)
- Discuss feelings. Encourage them to express their emotions in words (e.g., How does it feel when someone takes your toy that you are playing with?).
- A game you can play to get children to use more descriptive words, have a child reach into a bag to feel a mystery object. That child has to describe what the object feels like to the rest of the children.

FIGURE 7-6 43–48 Months Activities

Activities 3½ - 4 Years Continued

My Body Is Wonderful — Large & Small Muscle Activities

- Play favorite small group games where the children can learn to take turns, such as *Duck Duck Goose* (see Figure 7-7).
- Set up more difficult manipulative centers that help improve fine motor movement. You can have them sort, stack, count, or play with smaller items than before (smaller beads, small plastic chain links, etc.).
- Set up "soft areas" where the children can try a somersault down a foam wedge or on a mat. Allow children to explore what they can do; the cushion is there in case they need it.
- Play creative yet simple tag games outdoors or gymnasium. Everyone must hop like a frog, baby crawl, or gallop like a horse. A simple way to make sure everyone has a turn is to shout out a child's name and have everyone chase after that one child. Once they are caught, call out the next name of the person to chase. Make sure you let everyone have a turn.
- Encourage the children to climb on the jungle gym or swing. Make sure it is a safe height and they are closely supervised.
- Sing more songs and add various large and small movements. They would enjoy adding simple sign language to some familiar or new songs.

Category 3

- Set up a little basketball area with low hoops and encourage bouncing the ball and trying to shoot a basket. You can even use a laundry basket on the ground.
- Create picture cards of everyday objects that you use. Have one child look at a card and act out how they use the item. Let the other children guess what he is acting out (e.g., jump rope, spoon, popsicle, etc.).
- Set up a net outside in the grass to give the children a target when they kick a ball.
- Let the children pour their own drink at snack time. Provide a small pitcher and mark the glass to prevent spills.
- Have a picnic lunch and allow the children to spread peanut butter and jelly on bread to make their own sandwich.
- Teach children to do some simple dances, such as the twist (twist your arms and waist in opposite directions) or the Charlie Brown (rock back and forth from the front foot to the back foot).
- Set out short obstacles for the children to jump over. Try to keep it at about 6 inches or shorter for this age.
- Make butter in a jar. Put heavy cream and a pinch of salt in a clean jar with a lid. Close the lid tightly and have the children shake it to make the butter. Have them take turns shaking because it takes a while. You may add yellow food coloring to make the butter yellow.
- There are many great children's CDs out there that have movement songs you can do with your children. *Kids in Motion* is a CD with songs called "Animal Action," where the children are asked to move like different animals.

FIGURE 7–6 43–48 Months Activities

Activities 3½ - 4 Years Continued

Creating My Way — Creative Exploration

- Make a necklace out of an "o" shaped cereal or candy that is safe for them to eat.
- Have the children practice cutting on straight, curvy, and zigzag lines. As they improve, provide shapes or pictures for them to cut.
- Create collages based on your theme. If you are talking about the zoo, have them cut out all the animals you might find in a zoo. If you are talking about the color blue, have them cut out anything they can find that is blue. After they cut, then have them paste them on thick paper.
- Make bubble paintings. Make a runny solution of non-toxic paint and soap. Place some of the paint solution in a small cup. Have the child blow into a straw in the cup to make bubbles. Either place paper under the cup or place the paper on top of the bubble to make bubble paintings.
- Have the children create treasure maps. Provide pencils, paper, crayons, and any other supplies to help draw a map.
- In Circle Time discuss different colors of skin, eyes, etc. Let each child use a mirror to look in and draw a picture of what they see. Point out eyes, nose, mouth, ears, hair, glasses, etc. Extend the activity with an art activity. Encourage them to use the special skin color crayons to color it in according to their own skin color. Post the pictures and share each child's.
- Make paper bag puppets according to your theme. If you are discussing the community, you may want to make a police officer puppet or doctor puppet. If you are discussing farms, you may want to make a pig or horse puppet.
- Have the children help create a colorful alphabet to decorate the room. Make a page with a giant bubble letter for the whole alphabet. Give them various materials to fill the letter in, such as buttons, small beads, paper scraps, or rice. Let them color on blank paper without guidelines. Just let them be as creative as they want to be.
- Give them paint mixed with glitter to paint sparkly pictures that will glisten in the sun. Have them help make a giant sun for the wall. Cut out a large sun shape and have them work together to paint it with yellow and orange glitter-filled paint.
- Make sock puppets. Give the children a plain, white sock and have them draw a face on the end of the sock with a fabric marker.
- Create smelly pictures by adding a spice, such as cinnamon, to paint.
- Cut sponges in different shapes that relate to your theme. Let the children dip these sponges into paint to make prints of the shape on paper. You can use this paper to cover a bulletin board while you work on the theme (e.g., cut moons and stars out for animals that are awake in the nighttime).
- Let the children use glue to draw on cardstock. Encourage them to draw shapes or letters with glue and then have them sprinkle colored sand or glitter on the glue and then shake the extra off. For easier cleanup have them shake the extra sand or glitter onto a paper plate or tray that you can put back in the containers to be used again.
- Discuss different colors of hair and textures (curly hair vs. straight). Provide the children a yarn color that closely matches their hair color so they can glue it on pictures of faces to create a self-portrait. Label the portraits with each child's name Hang them up and use them as "teachable moments" throughout the next week.

Category

4

FIGURE 7–6 43–48 Months Activities

Activities 3½ - 4 Years Continued

Exploring Our World — Activities to Explore Cognitive, Pre-Math, Sensory, and Science

- Dig up some worms and dirt, and then put them in a clear container for the children to observe. Be sure to return the worms to the ground at the end of the day, so you don't have to explain why the worms don't move anymore.
- Encourage and help children count how many times they can hop or jump.
- In a sand box or outdoor sand table, give the children buckets, shovels, and other toys to help them create. Try giving them a few buckets of water and explore what happens to sand when it is wet.
- Use the colorful counting bears to work on some different skills. Give directions such as make a line of bears and put the blue bear first, take 4 bears out of the bucket, or sort the bears by color.
- Play the mirror game. Tell the children, "Do what I do." Then make different hand movements and/or facial expressions. They then mirror what you do. You can always end by placing your hands in your lap so they are calm and ready to listen.
- Play guessing games with food. Provide a variety of common foods with a distinct smell. Hide the food or have the children cover their eyes and smell the food. Have them try and guess the smell. You can use the same idea with taste, too.
- Purchase or create pair puzzles. This means there are only two pieces to the puzzle and a picture on each piece is related. You can make puzzles with opposites, shapes, or rhyming words (e.g., one piece has a picture of an empty glass and the other piece has a picture of a full glass).

Category

5

- Make a weather bear (or other animal). Laminate the bear and different weather related clothing, and then put velcro on them so the children can dress the bear according to the weather (e.g., if it is raining outside, then the children can put a raincoat and rain boots on the bear). This is a great activity to do everyday.
- Give the children a chance to compare weights of different or same objects such as several different blocks that they can compare. Change the objects you use on a regular basis to provide a variety of practice. Use the seasons to guide your weight and size selections such as (several sizes of pumpkins during Fall).
- Create cards of different shaped objects and then make the silhouette of that object. Have the children match the object and its silhouette.
- Make 5-10 cut outs of each different shape. You can make them a variety of sizes and colors. Make a corresponding envelope for each shape. Have the children sort the shapes into the envelopes.
- Make a die of colors out of a small cardboard box (make sure it is a cube shape). Use a different color on each of the six sides. Have the children take turns rolling the die and telling what color they rolled.
- Set a tightly sealed ant farm out at the science table for the children to observe.
- Discuss animals and the different names for their babies (e.g., cow – calf, dog – puppy, bear - cub, pig – piglet, etc.).
- Do a sky watch. Take your blankets out and lay on the ground during recess. Discuss what they see. Later extend the activity encourage painting, drawing or use of paper scraps to cut and glue what they observed.

FIGURE 7–6 43–48 Months Activities

really are their friends! Exploring three-year-olds need redirection at times. If a child is climbing on the stove in the housekeeping center (discovering his own leverage), redirect him or her to the climbing apparatus or to the foam blocks, which can be used as steps.

My Body Is Wonderful includes large-muscle activities involving large muscles in arms, legs, and body and fine-motor activities for the children to develop hand and finger movements and eye–hand coordination. Some of the planned activities involve physical games that appeal to preschool children. The Large-Muscle Games Activities are described in detail on Figure 7–7. Be sure to choose adequate space for large-muscle activities. *If children are crowded or made to wait a long time for a turn, they may become aggressive.* Conversely if too much open space is available, children are tempted to run from one end to the other. Rotate the activities on a regular basis presenting new and different experiences.

CREATING MY WAY

Creating My Way activities offers a variety of art and creative activities for the children. Art activities are opportunities for the children to explore various mediums, they must be open-ended, offering a variety of experiences involving the senses and providing for children functioning at different levels. Bredekamp and Copple (1997) guide us with developmentally appropriate practice advice and encourage us to provide "children daily opportunities for aesthetic expression and appreciation through art" (p. 32). Provide the children ample time and frequent opportunities to freely explore various mediums. Adequate time periods allow children to become more deeply involved in their creations, if they choose. Avoid the use of dittos and keep teacher-prepared projects at a minimum. Prepare the materials and offer simple explanations for their use. Teachers observe for guidance if necessary, replenish the materials, and assist with writing the child's name and displaying. Offer children the choice to participate in the art activity or to wait until they are ready. Given a variety of materials and the opportunity to explore, children will become involved as their interest and ability levels dictate.

Art is not created for the parents' benefit; it is created for the development of the child's creative abilities. To that end, you can help families understand, through training, that artwork coming from your room will not have "teacher-produced" parts nor color-inside-the-line projects. Early care and education professionals are also aware that art is also not for the advantage of the teacher, or just to provide decorations for the classroom wall space. There is more value to be gained by the children exploring a variety of art media (process) expressed individually than creating identical pictures that suit the adult's interpretation of what the art "should" look like when finished (product). Art is for the child to explore his or her environment with color, textures, etc.

At first the art experience is simply cause and effect. For example, "If I do this with the paint brush, I will make a colored mark on the paper" or "This feels a certain way in my hands, and I can move it in different ways." Children will get more involved in the exploration and creation with the materials as they are given the opportunity to work with them. When the work is completed and ready to display, hang the children's work at their eye level so they can see it and talk about it. They also can locate it to show it to others. Cover the art display area with a large piece of thick plastic available in discount or fabric stores, so it won't matter how often the children touch the artwork. Let the child determine if he wants to save his work, hang it, take it home, or throw it away.

Use art to further the daily learning experiences such as an opportunity to begin literacy skill building for this age group. Ask the child to tell a story about her creation while you write their story on a 3- by 5-inch card or a storyboard. Place the child's name on everything she creates so she will recognize her name in print. Be sure to date all the work. Start an art portfolio in September through June, and watch the children's abilities leap forward!

LARGE-MUSCLE GAME ACTIVITIES

Duck, Duck, Goose: Directions

Have the children sit in a circle facing each other. One child is "it" and walks around the circle. As "it" walks around, "it" taps the children's heads and calls them "duck" or "goose." When "it" taps a child's head and says "goose," then that child chases "it" around the circle. The object is for "it" to go around the circle and sit in "goose's" spot without being tagged by "goose." Then "goose" becomes "it" and play continues in the same way. As children get older, then you can have "it" sit in the middle of the circle if he is tagged by "goose." "It" must stay in the middle until another person tagged replaces them.

Monkey in the Middle: Directions

This game is usually played with three children. You need a ball that the children can toss and catch easily. One person is the monkey and they stand in the middle of the other two children. Those two children stand 15–20 feet apart (or more as the children become stronger) and play a simple game of toss and catch with each other. The "monkey" tries to interrupt their game by getting the ball when it is dropped or while it flies through the air. If the "monkey" gets the ball, then the person who last touched the ball becomes the new "monkey" in the middle. Play continues in the same manner. You can add variations, such as having two "monkeys" in the middle or by having the children pass a bean bag back and forth.

Hopscotch: Directions

Hopscotch is played outside on the blacktop or inside a gross motor room. You first make a series of squares in a line as shown below. (There are many variations of this design or you can make up your own series.) The children can jump from one square to the next on one foot or they can jump with one foot down when there is one square and two feet when two squares are next to each other. You can even have the children use a pebble or checker to throw into a square, jump to it following the rules, and then jump back. These are just a few ways to play this game or the children can just use the squares to practice hopping back and forth on one or two feet.

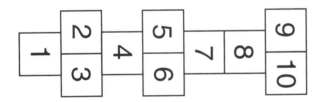

Mother, May I: Directions

Line the children up against a wall or on a line at one side of the playing area. Have the children face you and you stand 15–30 feet away, depending on the age of the children. One at a time ask a child by name to do a certain kind of step or jump and the number of times they are to do it (e.g., Marcus, take 5 baby steps forward or Allie, take 2 leaps forward). Before the child can do the command, they must ask, "Mother, may I?" Then you answer, "Yes, you may." Then the child takes those steps. If they forget to ask, then the child must go back to the starting line. Play continues down the line in this manner until one child crosses the finish line where you are standing.

Here are some possible steps you can have the children take (or you can make up your own):
- Scissor steps—one foot crosses over in front of the other foot, then you cross that foot over the one you just moved
- Baby step—step with one foot right in front of the other, heel to toe
- Giant leap—leap from one foot as far as possible
- Bunny hop—hop with both feet together
- Frog leap—jump the way a frog does
- Side steps—stand side ways and take a step sideways

FIGURE 7–7 Large Muscle Activities

A variety of Creating My Way activities for sensory, creative, and discovery activities are provided in Figure 7–8. Creating My Way activities offer basic ideas, alternative uses for materials, and suggestions for expanding basic activities. Additionally, tips for setting up materials and suggestions ensuring safe use of the materials are noted on Figure 7–8. Ideas for painting and use of crayons and markers are given as well as basic information on collages, sticker designs, chalk drawings, carpentry, and feely art bags.

A collection of recipes for sensory and creative expressions are available on Figure 7–9. Often, it is much less expensive to make basic materials than to purchase them. Included are recipes for different types of paint and play dough, bubble mix, chalk, and paste.

Refer back to Figure 2–2 to review the supplies and equipment appropriate for this age level. This is not intended as an all-inclusive list or as required equipment and supplies. The list does include items for the ideas suggested throughout *KIDEX for Threes* and a variety of equipment that would support well-planned interest centers. Many of the activities listed require supplies that can be provided by the teacher, using found or donated items. Costs can be kept lower with such materials, and parents often like to help by collecting materials such as old milk cartons, egg containers, expired magazines, etc. The opportunity to contribute promotes family involvement, and the children are often quite proud when their family collects and donates helpful materials to their class.

EXPLORING MY WORLD

Exploring My World will entice preschool children to experience and explore the world in which they live. The five senses are used for sensory exploration and learning about the world. Although sensory elements are essentially integrated in all of the KIDEX planned activities, they are grouped in this section to assist with planning a balanced program. Using sensory skills to teach concepts relating to size, measurement (math), floating, sinking, hard, soft, and other scientific concepts exploration will appeal to their curious nature as they open up to the exciting beginning of lifelong learning.

FUN WITH LANGUAGE AND TELLING TALES

A teacher will have a very important influence in the development of language and the introduction of books for young children. It is essential to remember that children understand a great deal of spoken language before they are able to use it themselves. At the beginning of language development, children first understand spoken language and then they associate names to objects. At about 24–30 months they start to combine two or three words (e.g., "no play now"). This is the time they really start to blossom and expand their vocabularies. At about 30–36 months, children begin to express tenses such as "I played dolls" versus "I play dolls." Their use of sentence structures begins to grow. They may start to carry on conversations of two or three sentences. By the time most children reach their third birthday, they are well on their way to using words that describe feelings, fears, and desires. There is quite an explosion in their growing use of words. They will not use perfect sentence structures, and if you listen closely they often leave out some of the sounds. Some may occasionally stutter or place the words out of order simply because their minds are moving faster than their ability to speak. If you ask a question, allow a child plenty of time to respond. Some children need more time to formulate their answers than others. Your pause will give them time to gather their thoughts and choose the words they wish to share.

Children learn language by listening to the sounds other humans make. They need to hear talking and the use of descriptive language around them. Talk with, sing with, and read to the children every day. Children need to be surrounded by language. Engaging them in conversations gives them opportunities to practice using their ever-expanding vocabulary. Talk about what you are doing together; speak to each child about his special

Creating My Way
Tips for Creative Expression

Here is a variety of tips to use for general guidance to set up and guide art and creative activities for the children. Refer to Figure 7–9 for a variety of recipes.

Finger-painting

Prepare a dishpan of soapy water for quick, close clean up. Some children will have a hard time getting started. This is messy work and they may not like it, especially if parents have drilled on maintaining clean hands. You might get them started with just one or two fingers until they're comfortable. Show the children different ways of using their hands: one or two fingers, palms, sides of hands in swirling motion, fingernails.

Finger-paint with shaving cream on the table top (supervision needed to see that the children don't get it in their eyes). You can sprinkle in a little water if the shaving cream gets too stiff. You can also add a bit of liquid tempera. You can make a print of a child's work by simply placing a piece of paper on his area and rubbing over it. You can finger-paint in cookie trays.

■ Finger-paint with pudding (use different flavors to provide new colors and tastes on different days).

■ You can also use yogurt or whipped cream.

■ Finger-paint to music.

■ Let the children mix two colors of finger-paint.

Brush painting tips for threes

■ Start with plain water so they can understand the basic concept.

■ Limit the number of children.

■ Use smocks.

■ Protect the floor/table/walls.

■ Use wide brushes and, if necessary, shorten the handles to approximately 6 inches, or buy ½-inch brushes with 6-inch handles at a hardware store (trim brushes).

■ Easels attached to walls provide for permanent areas, cannot be tipped over, and should have a washable surface behind them—or attach paper directly to a washable surface and attach paint trays directly to wall also. (For example, take a wide strip of thick vinyl, staple to the wall, and place a contrasting strip of vinyl to provide a border.)

■ Nontip paint trays should be used—you can make wood or cardboard cup holders. Baby food jars or cans can be used for the paint. Cut a hole in a sponge slightly smaller than the jar but leave "edges." This will hold the jar and catch drips as well.

■ Start with just one or two colors, progress to more colors and mixing colors and adding white to experiment.

■ Paint outdoors: Use water and large paint brushes to develop crossing mid-line by making big /, \, X, O, and any other shapes to promote the development of left-to-right movements.

Other painting implements

Roll top deodorant bottles (empty + clean), small pieces of sponge held with a spring-type clothes pin, cotton-tipped swabs, toothbrushes, feathers (wash with soap and water and a small amount of bleach).

Suggested surfaces to explore

Newsprint, newspaper—classifieds, shelf paper, butcher paper, grocery sacks, paper plates, Styrofoam trays (large) with paper glued inside, long strips of paper vs. rectangular, pellon.

Prepare an area for drying the paintings (clothesline works fine)

FIGURE 7–8 "Creating My Way" Tips for Creative Expression

Other ideas

- Use colored paper and only black and white paint
- **Salt painting:** the child can sprinkle salt on his painting before it is dry
- **Sponge painting:** Sponges are cut into various shapes (enough for various colors) and dipped into a shallow paint substance and then used to print on paper. Remind the child that he doesn't need to dip the sponge each time. If the child decides to smear the paint around with the sponge, that is how he has decided to use it!

Crayons/markers

Basic ideas for preschool children:

- Provide a large variety of colors to select from including various shades that represent the various colors of skin found in different ethnic groups.
- Use large pieces of paper and tape them to the surface
- Place a few crayons or water color markers in a container for each child. *When each child has his own supplies, fighting occurs less often.*
- Show children how to use crayons on their sides
- Band 2 crayons together for a different effect.
- **Preparing markers for use:** Water-soluble markers are wonderful fun for their brilliancy. Children should be supervised, however, so they don't suck the ends, or place the caps in their mouths. To prevent problems with caps, mix up plaster of Paris and put it in an old container. **(Dispose of any excess in the trash as it will harden in pipes.)** Immerse the marking-pen tops in the plaster of Paris and let the substance harden. The children can then return the markers to the tops, and one danger is removed! (Get rid of the caps.)

Collages

Provide a base (piece of newspaper, construction paper, cardboard for heavier items); a tray with a thin layer of glue (or use paste recipe included in recipe section); and the things to glue (e.g., scraps of paper children have torn (include different thicknesses); fabric scraps; Styrofoam; old greeting cards; string, yarn, and ribbon; nylon netting; macaroni in various shapes and colors; cotton balls). Children can dip the items in the glue, use cotton-swabs to spread the glue, or dip their fingers in the paste and spread it. Children can create a mural in this same manner. Tape a long sheet of paper to the table or on the wall for better visualization.

Sticker Designs

Place purchased stickers and bits of decorated contact paper on trays. Show the children how to peel the stickers and contact paper off and make a collage. Save wildlife and other interesting stamps that come in the mail, and show the children how to wet these (place one wet sponge between two children) and use them for collages.

Chalk Drawing

Cover the children's work surface. Wet the paper and give them large, nontoxic chalks. (Recipe for chalk included in Figure 7–9.

Use different shapes of paper for the various activities listed, just to add variety or to highlight a holiday.

Beginning Carpentry

Let the children use Styrofoam (blocks, sheets, pieces) and golf tees (with points blunted with sandpaper) and a plastic hammer. They can also use a large lump of play dough in the same manner.

Feely art

Fill resealable freezer bags with one of the following; toothpaste (variety of colors), shaving cream, lotion, pudding. Feel the bags and talk about them; cool the bags and talk about them. After the children have experimented with the different bags, hang them on the wall, and the children can continue to manipulate the materials during center time.

FIGURE 7–8 *"Creating My Way" Tips for Creative Expression (Continued)*

Recipes

Basic Finger-Paint

Use purchased washable, nontoxic finger-paint or make your own (much less expensive):

Combine 2 cups flour and ¼ cup of water. (This mixture should be thick like glue.)

Add a few drops of food color.

Each child needs only 2 or 3 tablespoons.

Brush Paint

Basic recipe (less expensive than purchased paint)

1 cup bentonite mixed with 2 quarts hot water

Allow mixture to sit in a lidded container for 2–3 days, stirring each day (it will not be smooth initially).

When the bentonite becomes smooth, divide the mix into smaller jars.

Mix in 3 or more tablespoons of dry tempera in each jar and stir.

Add paint as needed for hue, and water to smooth it.

Store in covered jars.

Play Dough

The children can help you make this!

Mix:

¼ cup of vegetable oil

1½ cups of flour

½ cup of salt

Approx. ¼ cup of water

Color with a few drops of food coloring.

Knead (good exercise for little fingers) until you have a smooth mix and the color is even.

Add more flour or water as necessary.

Put in an air-tight container (e.g., metal can with plastic top—be sure to check the can edges). Storing in a plastic bag is not advised, as the dough will be too wet.

Change the texture of the dough by adding rice, salt, cornmeal, etc.

Edible Play Dough

½ cup powdered milk

½ cup wheat germ

1 cup peanut butter

¼ cup honey

Stir all together, adding more powdered milk if mixture is too sticky.

Bubble Mix

2 tablespoons dishwashing detergent

1 tablespoon glycerin

1 cup water

Change amounts as need. Some detergents will work better than others. Add food coloring if you wish. Use plastic or pipe cleaner hoop blowers or fly swatters dipped in a tray of soap.

FIGURE 7–9 Recipes

Paste Recipes

1. Mix:

½ cup water

1 cup flour

2. Wheat paste

Mix:

1½ cups of boiling water

½ teaspoon salt

2 teaspoons of wheat flour

Store in a covered jar.

Hint: To keep the lids of storage jars from sticking, rub petroleum jelly around the edge.

Chalk

Mix:

2 tablespoons powdered tempera paint

3 tablespoons of plaster of paris

½ cup of water

Let mixture harden in a small paper cup for approximately one hour.

Remove the cup for good chunky chalk.

You can make your own chalkboards too—toddler size! Take a large piece of cardboard, and spray it with several coats of chalkboard paint (from paint stores or hobby shops). Once it is dry, you can "seal" the edges with colored tape.

FIGURE 7–9 Recipes *(Continued)*

qualities, talk about situations, share what you're going to do next. Use a variety of means to continue to expose preschool children to language development opportunities.

Early care and education professionals are well aware that reading helps develop children's attention span, builds vocabularies, enhances self-esteem, increases the ability to visualize and imagine, and provides many opportunities to understand words and how they create the spoken language. The introduction of books is an essential element in your overall language program.

LANGUAGE BUILDING, READING, AND SINGING

Reading to children for as little as 15–20 minutes per day from an early age contributes to a myriad of positive brain developments. Preschool children are like little sponges soaking up information from all sources. They love to look at books and hear stories read to them. They are especially fond of books that describe stories they can relate to their own life. For example, stories such as grocery shopping, visiting grandparents, taking a bath, and helping around the house or school are stories they can delight in hearing. Simple little books with pictures allow them to read stories by themselves. Stories with rhyming words and repetitive phrases appeal to young children. They are interested in examples of similarities and differences. Simple finger plays and songs are something they can begin to memorize and repeat. Plan on at least five to six books per child in each room and at least two copies each of favorites. Choose a variety of books with real people and real pictures reflecting diversity, antibias attitudes, and multiethnic representation. The following books are good choices for three-year-olds:

The Big Fat Worm by Nancy Van Laan
The Biggest Truck by David Lyon
Color Zoo by Lois Ehlert
Follow Me! by Mordicai Gerstein
Gregory, the Terrible Eater by Mitchell Sharmat
It's Mine! by Leo Lionni
Rat-a-Tat, Pitter Patter by Alan Benjamin
"Quack!" Said the Billy-Goat by Charles Causley
Tails, Toes, Eyes, Ears, Nose by Marilee Robin Burton
The Wing on a Flea by Ed Emberley

Although young children are comforted by repetition, preschool children have imaginations that are beginning to grow and they will often begin to enjoy variations in one of their regular stories. For instance they may find it humorous to hear the story of "Goldilocks and the Three Bears" changed to the "Boy with the Black Hair and the Three Ducks." Flannel board stories bring the concept alive, and the preschool child can easily participate in telling the story. Extend the reading activity into the dramatic play area by encouraging the children to act out the story characters or give them opportunities to create art using the story as their theme, crayons and paint as their medium.

Singing and playing songs on a regular basis is yet another excellent opportunity for practicing language skill development. Music and singing offers opportunities to explore sound and to assist with building and mastering language skills. Music and singing are a vital part of any curriculum and promote many positive influences in environments inhabited by young children. Set up a tape recorder for the children to have plenty of opportunities to hear their own voices.

Nursery rhymes are also an enjoyable activity to incorporate into the day. Many nursery rhymes are very old and date as far back as the 14th century. As three-year-olds continue to mature, they become quite capable of memorizing and repeating nursery rhymes and songs. There are a multitude of books on the market, found in libraries, bookstores, and Web sites such as Scholastic Book Clubs (http://www.scholastic.com). An extensive Web site of the most popular nursery rhymes lists "Lost Lyrics of Old Nursery Rhymes—112 Additional Online Nursery Rhymes, History and their Origins!" at http://www.rhymes.org.

TRANSITION ACTIVITIES: PREPARING TO CHANGE ACTIVITIES

Transitions are periods of time in a program that allow for passing from one activity to another. Transitions occur on a regular basis every day in a program. If deliberate transitions are not built into the day, changing activities can lead to confusion and chaos. Every early care educator understands children are comforted with routines built into their day. Establishing consistent transition routines will help them close an activity and move to another smoothly. Planned transitions built in the program day provide adequate time for children to participate with ending their activity rather than autocratically demanding they abruptly end the activity without warning. Signal them a few minutes before a change in activities, and they will be more responsive. Offering transition time helps in changing from one activity to the next with the least amount of protest.

Very young children cannot be expected to sit and wait for extended periods of time. Teach the children to sing or chant along with you as you are preparing their lunch table or preparing for outside play. Use a simple song or chant, and use a tune over and over. Choose words in your song or chant to gain their attention and to describe what you hope to accomplish. The rhythm of chant or song will provide a distraction and ease the transition. Some suggestions for transition activities for young children are:

1. Have a puppet used only for giving directions. Use different voices to interest the children. This method appeals to auditory and visual learners.

2. Giving simple fun directions such as "Find your rug (each child has his own rug sample) and sit down and wiggle your feet" or "wave your hands" or point to body parts.

3. Invite helpers to assist you to set up for the next activity.

4. After ringing a bell, hold up a picture of the next activity so that the children see what is next, and they may even proceed more quietly to that area.

5. Dismiss children one at a time for the next activity, talk about something they are wearing (e.g., If you are wearing a green dress, you may go to a center).

6. Make funny noises and faces, and see if the children can mimic you.

7. Develop a broad repertoire of finger plays and songs, including clapping, marching, and other movement. A good example of a "singing game": "Can you do what I do, I do, I do? Can you do what I do, just like me?"

8. Imagine you are on a bus (or plane, in a car, on a bicycle, a butterfly's wings), and have each child ride with you to the lunch table.

9. Offer books of all kinds—children can sit wherever they want.

10. Play specific music used only for transition times. The children will begin to associate the particular tune with a sense that time is drawing near to end this activity.

At the end of the chapter several books are listed under recommended resources for more transition idea activities. A variety of well-planned transition activities employed on a regular basis will promote safety and reduce stress for all parties involved.

GUIDANCE

Any time a group of children or individuals form a group, it is natural to experience occasional misunderstandings or conflicting views. A young child is at the threshold of learning how his or her behavior and decisions affect themselves and those around them. They have limited experience interacting with people and their environment. Therefore the decisions and choices they make will reflect their limited ability to solve problems in a situation. They are often motivated by intense desires to explore interesting opportunities or to take control of items others possess, simply because they want it! If they lack appropriate activities planned for their age level or are forced to sit extended periods of time beyond their expected limits, they are bound to become bored and act out their frustrations.

In a developmentally appropriate atmosphere, the early child educator offers a myriad of techniques and solutions to guide each child through the complicated process of learning self-discipline and cooperation in the group. As with peeling an onion, there are many layers, and the goal takes many years for young children to achieve. The preschool child is now more capable of practicing cooperation than earlier and benefits from steady exposure to appropriate guidance.

To create a safe atmosphere that fosters respect for the children and materials in the room, the preschool teacher must provide direction and awareness. Know what is happening everywhere with everyone. Redirection, clarifying feeling, and guided choices are effective techniques. Use redirection techniques through the use of distraction. "Kent, here is some play dough and a hammer. Why don't you build a house over here?" instead of "Kent, quit hitting the cubbies with that block." Draw them away from the point of controversy, offering another idea or choice (substitution) such as "Martha, would you like to help bathe this doll?" instead of "Stop playing in the water fountain!" If they are frustrated with another person or a situation, help them clarify their feelings by offering words they can use to describe how they feel about a situation. "Tell Horst you feel angry he took your book." Certain behaviors cannot be allowed, such as hurting another, risky climbing, and endangering themselves or others, and will need quick automatic consequences. Usually a skillful and observant teacher will see a situation brewing and intercede before it escalates.

Create clear rules everyone can follow. Make sure the children understand them, and follow through consistently with consequences once they are established. Avoid empty threats or an action you can't or won't do. Take the time to establish three or four simple rules stated in positive language. Try these: (1) Respect other people's bodies and feelings. (2) Respect belongings and materials. (3) Clean up your own mess. (4) Make safe choices. When a rule is broken or about to be, remind the child of the rule. If the behavior continues, take the child aside, make sure the children understand them and follow through consistently with consequences that are developmentally appropriate for the age of the child. For instance, "Faizaan, you are welcome to play with the blocks once you put away the crayons you used."

Professional periodicals, educational magazines, early childhood workshops, and active affiliation with organizations who promote developmentally appropriate practices are areas where an early care and education professional will find a wealth of knowledge concerning appropriate guidance. It is remarkable to observe a skilled professional guide a group of children with effective planning, understanding, praise, conflict management, and redirection. Learning to provide effective guidance is a skill that deserves continuous training and practice and is always time well spent!

PERSONAL SUPPLY INVENTORY CHECKLIST

If your center depends on the children's families to provide supplies, use the personal supply inventory sheet to communicate when supplies need replenishing (example in Figure 7–8). Form a habit of reporting the individual inventory once a week. Notify your clients when their child's supplies are low. Planning ahead will decrease the inconvenience caused by completely depleting needed supplies. Routinely inventory supplies on Thursday or Friday. This allows busy families to shop over the weekend.

RECORDING OBSERVATIONS OF THE THREE-YEAR-OLD CHILD'S DAY

Once children reach preschool age, some centers decide to record daily information as a class group rather than individually. Other centers are mandated by licensing rules to create an individual record for each child. Two options are offered here for daily recordkeeping.

In Chapter 3, "Establishing an Excellent Path for Communication," a completed example of the Three-Year-Old Daily Observation Sheet was reviewed. In this chapter, select the blank template for the Three-Year-Old Daily Observation Sheet, located in the Forms and Templates Appendix for your daily use. Keep a written daily record for each child. Accurate

PERSONAL SUPPLY INVENTORY CHECKLIST

CHILD'S NAME: _Martin (Enter Last Name)_   **DATE:** _May XX, XXXX_

SUPPLY	FULL	HALF	NEED MORE
Disposable trainers		✓	✓
Plastic pants covers			
Underwear			
Shirts			
Long pants			
Short pants			✓
Socks			✓
Diapers			
Disposable wipes		✓	✓
Waterproof paper for diaper barrier (such as wax paper)	✓		
Diaper ointment	✓		
Other:			

FIGURE 7–8 Personal Supply Inventory Checklist

recording in a timely manner gives the family a clear understanding of their child's day. Adopting a routine for recording assures that all-important aspects are covered. Provide parents with a copy of this record so they, too, will have a record of their child's rest time patterns, toileting patterns or diaper changes, eating patterns, medications, rest time patterns, and any important observations that day. Consider creating the Three-Year-Old Daily Observation Sheet on two-part forms: Provide one for the parents/guardians at departure. File the second copy for at least a couple of months or longer if your state requires. The second copy is useful for referring to in parent conferences and in tracking normal patterns and any possible unusual occurrences in their day.

The other method mentioned involves recording information for the group only and reporting it using the Current Events Bulletin Board. Examples of the Eating Patterns (Figure 3–13), Resting Time Patterns (Figure 3–14), and Our Days (Figure 3–12) were provided in Chapter 3, "Establishing an Excellent Path for Communication." Use these charts in place of the Three-Year-Old Daily Observation Sheet. All the pertinent information is covered by duplicating the templates and updating the Current Events Bulletin Board daily. This information is very helpful to parents, because it may well affect the way they plan dinner for their child or schedule their bedtime hour. For example, if lunch didn't appeal to a child, he may need to eat dinner early or have a light snack before dinner. The parents will appreciate the time you take in providing this information. For some children the information may remain fairly routine; for others, it may even affect them the next day if they haven't had a good nap the day before and didn't get enough sleep that night.

Although most children potty-train by age three, as mentioned previously, a few may lag in this area due to immaturity or delayed developmental capacity. Refer to the Forms and Templates Appendix for a blank template used to record Toilet Training Progress and for a blank template to record Diaper Changing data. Examples of the how to fill out the Toilet Training and Diaper Changing sheet were covered in Chapter 3 under Figure 3–7 and Figure 3–8.

Regardless of how you choose to report the daily observations, keep a copy of the written observations to review in the event questions occur or a conference is warranted. Occasionally parents/guardians express concerns first. Their child's appetite may fluctuate, or their child's rest-time patterns may interfere with their nighttime schedule. A collection of past information provides the center staff with a mechanism needed to answer their concerns and reach mutually acceptable outcomes. The director is encouraged to review all records at least monthly to look for consistent behavior or spot areas where intervention or training is warranted. Before you leave for lunch or at the end of your shift, check the charts for accuracy. Remember, even after your shift ends your observations and information provide pertinent information for parents' questions with regard to their child's care. An accurate record is essential to facilitate open communication!

COMPLETING A NEW CHILD TRANSITIONING REPORT

The details of how a new child is adjusting to the program is of primary importance to their families and the director of the center. Typically a child attending for two weeks full time will bond with the center, staff, and children even in the most difficult circumstances. It may take a little longer for some, or if the child attends on a part-time basis. An example of the completed New Child Transitioning Report was reviewed on Figure 3–15 in Chapter 3. Establishing an Excellent Path for Communication. Although some of this information is already recorded on the class listings, the families will find an individual copy helpful to share with other family members during this period of adjustment.

Make a duplicate copy of the blank template New Child Transitioning Report found in the Appendix, and complete a report for each new child in your group. Indicate the day each child is in attendance, if they played with the learning materials, or if they participated in activities some, a lot, or not yet. How was the child's appetite today? Indicate whether it was light, partial, or complete for all applicable meals. Record the times the child fell asleep and awoke from the nap. If they are using diapers, record their bowel and bladder patterns. If they are toilet-training, attach a copy of their Toileting Training Progress Sheet to the New Child Transitioning Report. Report whether they had a fair day or great day. If you have any questions about care, this is a good place to communicate the need for clarification. If the child cried most of the day, it is important not to dwell on the subject. It's essential to share an honest account, yet it can be beneficial to focus on the positive progress such as they did not cry as often, they seemed to observe more. Perhaps she did not join in group activities yet, but she did seem interested and curious. Using this approach is more comforting to a parent racked with guilt rather than hearing, "Oh, she just cried all day long!"

ENDING THE DAY WITH EACH CHILD: DEPARTURE

There are many details to attend to as children leave the program. Help the parents or guardians gather each child's art activities, medications, ointments, blankets, and personal belongings, thus promoting a pleasant transition. If time permits, briefly review the Daily Observation Sheet with them or direct them to the Current Events Bulletin Board for group information, and add any special observations you might have noted that day. Try to share with parents a positive encounter from the day. Families who consistently receive negative reports will learn to avoid encounters with you.

As you are well aware, young children require a great deal of time and energy. The parents have often spent a long day fulfilling the obligations required of their career. Although they are very pleased to see their child, they often have an accumulation of stress from their day. Your pleasant attitude and helpful manner assist them in making a smooth exit from the center, and allows for the highest and best outcome for all involved.

Prepare your room for the next day. Tidy up and finalize the tasks on the cleaning list. As you bring your day to a close, take a few moments to appreciate yourself. You have touched many lives today by creating a safe and secure environment for children to play and learn. Your efforts have made it possible for parents and guardians to leave their children, with the confidence they are well cared for, so they in turn can provide for their families. You are a vital link to the safekeeping of children in your community, and your efforts have made a profound difference.

NURTURING THE NURTURERS

Working with young children can be very physically and emotionally demanding work. It requires a great deal of understanding and patience as they journey through their task of unfolding. A wise teacher learns to recognize when it is time to take a break and replenish his or her energy reserves. It is amazing how a small break, planned on a regular basis, to experience a peaceful moment and regroup, can help you maintain a fresh perspective.

Continuing education, books, and workshops provide early care and teaching professionals with new information, different approaches for solving similar situations and opportunities to share with other professionals in meaningful ways. Seek support of professional organizations and the professional materials devoted to the early care and education field. It is always refreshing to learn new approaches to universal challenges.

Read humorous books on the subject, such as *Just Wait til You Have Children of Your Own!* by the beloved author Erma Bombeck. They can help restore a waning sense of humor and serve as a reminder you are not alone. You are very important to the early care and education community and the children you mind every day. A rested, well-informed teacher dedicated to the whole child's being has the best opportunity to promote positive life-long results for the children entrusted to him or her.

Recommended Resources

Alexander, N. P., Burton, R., Dall, J., Miller, & Owens, C. (2001). *Circle time activities.* Lincolnwood, IL: Publications International.

Allison, L. (1994). *Razzle dazzle doodle art.* Boston: Little, Brown.

Altman, R. (1994). *Jump, wiggle, twirl, & giggle!* New York: Random House.

Becker, J., Reid, K., Steinhaus, P., & Wieck, P. (1994). *ThemeStorming.* Beltsville, MD: Gryphon House.

Broad, L. P., & Butterworth, N. T. (1974). *The playgroup handbook.* New York: St. Martins Press.

Clark, A. (2003). *The ABC's of quality child care.* Clifton Park, NY: Thomson Delmar Learning.

Coletta, A. J., & Coletta, K. (1986). *Year 'round activities for three-year-old children.* West Nyack, NY: Center for Applied Research in Education.

Crary, E. (1993). *Without spanking or spoiling.* Seattle: Parenting Press.

Dibble, C. H., & Lee, K. H. (2000). *101 easy wacky crazy activities for young children.* Beltsville, MD: Gryphon House.

Feldman, J. (2000). *Rainy day activities.* Beltsville, MD: Gryphon House.

Fraiberg, S. H. (1987/1959). *The magic years.* New York: Fireside.

Garttrell, D. (2004). *The power of guidance.* Clifton Park, NY: Thomson Delmar Learning.

Gober, S. (2002). *Six simple ways to assess young children.* Clifton Park, NY: Thomson Delmar Learning.

Harms, J. M., & Lettow, L. (1996). *Picture books to enhance the curriculum.* New York: H.W. Wilson.

Herr, J. (1994). *Working with young children.* Tinley Park, IL: Goodheart-Willcox.

Kohl, M. F. (2000). *The big messy art book.* Beltsville, MD: Gryphon House.

Kostelnik, M., Soderman, A. & Whiren, A. (1993). *Developmentally appropriate programs in early childhood education.* New York: Merrill.

Lind, K. (2005). *Exploring science in early childhood education.* Clifton Park, NY: Thomson Delmar Learning.

Odeon, K. (1997). *Great books for girls.* New York: Ballantine Books.

Odeon, K. (1998). *Great books for boys.* New York: Ballantine Books.

Oser, A. (1997). *Star power for preschoolers.* St. Paul, MN: Redleaf Press.

Stephens, C. G. (2000). *Coretta Scott King award books.* Englewood, CO: Libraries Unlimited.

VanCleave, J. (1998). *Play and find out about math.* New York: Wiley.

Wilmes, D., & Wilmes, L. (1983). *Everyday circle times.* Elgin, IL: Building Blocks.

United Art & Education Equipment & Supplies. 1-800-322-3247, http://www.UnitedNow.com

To find your specific
State's Licensing, Rules
and Regulations go to:

http://nrc.uchsc.edu

CHAPTER 8

Educational Articles for Families & Staff

This chapter provides short educational articles about providing care and developing a better understanding of three-year-olds. Post these articles on the *current events bulletin board*, print them in program newsletters, or use them as basis for parenting and staff education classes. Store copies of these and other informative articles that you collect in the KIDEX class book for future reference.

The articles include Vision Screening, page 110; Learning From the Process Not the Outcome, page 111; Conducting A Cooking Class for Three-Year-Olds, page 112; Whining is a Form of Communication, page 113; Questions About Hearing for Young Children, page 114; When Does the Learning Start, page 115; and Pink Eye, page 116.

Read additional information on the following found in the KIDEX series:

KIDEX FOR INFANTS

Sudden Infant Death Syndrome
Colds
Respiratory Synctial Virus (RSV)
Strep Throat
Ear Infections
Diarrhea Illness
Diaper Rash
Convulsions/Seizures
Teething

KIDEX FOR ONES

Impetigo
Pinworms
Ringworm
Provide Toddler Safety
Help Prevent Choking
Is Sharing Possible for Toddlers
Biting Is a Toddler Affair

KIDEX FOR TWOS

Mashed Fingers
Chicken Pox
Scabies
Submersion and Drowning Accidents
Tooth Injuries
Temper Tantrums
Potty Training
Dental Care for Young Children

KIDEX FOR FOURS

Is My Child Ready for Kindergarten?
Healthy Floor Posture
Bedwetting
My Child is Shy
Signs of Child Abuse
Styles of Learning
My Child Stutters!

VISION SCREENING FOR YOUNG CHILDREN

Why do children need vision screening?

Vision problems affect one in twenty preschool children. Without early detection and treatment, it can impair their development, and possibly result in permanent vision loss if certain conditions are left untreated.

What are the signs of eye problems I should look for?

Look for signs of itching, such as rubbing the eyes, tilting the head, or squinting. Sometimes one eye will not track consistently with the other eye. The child might be at risk for amblyopia, a condition commonly known as "lazy eye".

Where can I go to get a screening?

The Prevent Blindness children's national screening program certifies volunteers to conduct screenings that will detect vision problems in preschool and school-age children. The screenings are accurate and help identify children who need further examination by an eye care professional. The screening program offers training sessions at no charge to communities that care for children, investigation such as child care centers.

Why are screenings important?

They are a cost-effective way to identify vision problems in children.

What happens during a screening?

The eye is examined to identify any outward symptoms of problems, such as watery eyes, swollen or crusty lids. The screener will also check the child's ability to see things from a distance.

How will I know if my child needs an eye exam?

Vision screening results are used to assess whether a child needs to see an eye doctor.

What if I can't afford to seek professional care for my child?

Programs are available to help families in financial need.

Recommended Resources:

Prevent Blindness America, http:// www.preventblindness.org

LEARNING FROM THE PROCESS NOT THE OUTCOME

How Come They Only Scribble? When Will It Look Like Art?

Story 1

Patty's Process Oriented Preschool

This is the story of two preschool experiences.

Lucy enters the front door of Patty's Process Oriented Preschool. She chooses the clay table as her first stop of the day. She learns about shape, texture, and conservation of matter. She strengthens the small muscles in her hands and develops eye-hand co-ordination and creativity. She learns science concepts and builds vocabulary. Next, Lucy visits the sensory table where she uses pumps, funnels, and cups to explore properties of water. She learns about volume, measurement, absorption, cause and effect relationships, and sink and float. The group comes together for a story about a bear family picnic. The bears eat toast with honey, strawberries, and lemonade. The children choose movement activities—bending, stretching, sequencing, following directions, and singing to "Teddy Bear, Teddy Bear" and "Going on a Bear Hunt". For snack, Lucy and her friends share toast with honey, strawberries, and lemonade. As they eat, they talk about the texture, tastes, and smells while the teacher records their descriptive words on a dry-erase board. They learn vocabulary, connect between spoken and written language, and they recognize letters from their names. After snack, Lucy, who loved the juicy, red strawberry, goes to the painting easel. She paints a giant red strawberry with a green leaf hat and tiny brown seeds in the shape of a smiling face. Lucy's next stop is the dramatic play center where, along with her friends, she takes the Teddy Bear family on a picnic. They sit together on the floor and reenact the story, using blocks for food. Later, she visits the math center and makes a picnic pattern with blue, red, and yellow bears sitting in a circle. Lunch was served picnic-style on a blanket in the back yard. Before rest time, Lucy reads the story of the bears' picnic to her baby doll. On her ride home, when her mother asks, "What did you do today?" Lucy does not say, "I mastered fourteen state kindergarten standards." Instead, she snuggles back in her car seat and smiles happily at her mother and says, "I had fun Mommy!" Mommy looks back at the hole in the knee of Lucy's tights, the smear of red paint on her arm, and the trace of sticky honey on her cheek and smiles, too.

Story 2

Pete Attends Cora's College Prep Project Preschool

He enters the front door and heads for a small table to do his morning work. He selects his name card and writes his name carefully on lined paper six times. He then traces dotted, outlined shapes. The children gather on the circle time carpet. The teacher reads them a story about a bear family picnic. After a snack of four saltines and four ounces of juice, it is art time. The children sit at two tables. "We will make strawberries today," Miss Bell tells them. The aid passes out strawberry-shaped cutouts and red crayons. "Color in only one direction," she reminds the children. When they finish coloring, the assistant drops a drip of glue at the top and gives each child a construction paper stem. Brown crayons are passed out to make seeds. Pete returns to the carpet area where Miss Bell explains about bears and what bears actually eat. Back at the tables, the children have a math lesson. Pete is handed a grid, and red and blue crayons. "We will make patterns today. Color the first square red, then blue, then red, then blue." At lunch, Pete talks with his friend and then goes outside to play on the slide with David and Molly. After a nap, it is time to go home. On the ride home, Pete's mother asks, "What did you do today?" Pete thinks for a minute. "We ate lunch and played outside." Peter watches the traffic through his window. His mother snuggles back in her seat and smiles at the receipts on the seat beside her. "You did these papers," Mommy reminds him.

Would you rather spend your day with Lucy or Pete? It is important to remember that we learn about children by how they explore their environment. Their simple trial-and-error efforts and discoveries are much more meaningful than any lecture or teacher-directed activity can provide. The adults in the classroom should act as facilitators, providing the children with what they need, and helping them to find answers to their questions. Look around your room to ensure you are offering many opportunities for divergent thinking, discovery, and exploration. You, too, can have a process-driven classroom.

CONDUCTING A COOKING CLASS FOR THREE-YEAR-OLDS

Where do I start?

The first step in conducting a cooking class for three-year-olds is to find a simple, fun recipe. Make sure it something where the children can do most of the work. Pick a recipe that the children can make without using the stove themselves. The children should be able to do all of the preparations and mixing without warming anything up. You may also want to try it out first on your own, just to make sure the recipe isn't too complicated.

What is a three-year-old capable of doing when it comes to cooking?

Not all children are capable of the same thing at the same age; however, there are several things that the average child can do. Most three-year-olds can help stir, shake, pour, and spread. They can also wrap and unwrap items or even crack nuts with a small hammer. You will want to make sure that when the child is pouring or stirring, the container is large enough to prevent spilling.

Are there any safety precautions I should take?

First of all, you should be sure the cooking area is clean. Disinfect the area and materials you are going to use. Also, have the children wash their hands before you start. Discuss with them the importance of keeping their hands clean while they are cooking, as well.

There are many dangers in a kitchen, so you may want to cook in a safe place in another room. Be sure to have another adult with you to take anything to and from the oven when needed. If any cutting or slicing is necessary, it's best that you do it beforehand. Keep the sharp knives and utensils away from the children.

What is the best way to set up when it is time to cook?

Read through the recipe to make sure that you have all the materials you will need. Set up measuring cups, bowls, ingredients, etc. on a tray or cart out of reach of the children. It is also a good idea to have a towel and trash can to clean up small spills.

When you are completely ready, have the children sit around a table. Be sure they all have a seat and are able to see what is going on. You will need to talk about what you are making. For example, if you are making play dough, then you will need to let them know that they cannot lick their fingers. As you begin cooking, make your way around the table, giving each child a chance to participate.

Where can I find good recipes?

There are many children's recipe books, magazines, and internet resources that have an abundance of ideas.

WHINING IS A FORM OF COMMUNICATION

Why does my three-year-old whine?

Preschool children experience moments and days of insecurity when they lack confidence. Their personality plays a part, and their level of sensitivity to change will effect how they react to new situations. Whining is an outward sign of the insecure feelings a child might be experiencing at the moment. Since a child's arrival, she or he has been growing by leaps and bounds, and whining is just one method of coping with all the changes the child is experiencing.

Is whining normal?

It is normal for three-year-olds to adopt a whining posture. Unfortunately, how whining effects the family also depends on their personalities and how sensitive they are to irritating sounds, such as a creaky hinge or a scratch on the chalkboard.

What can I do to stop this behavior?

It is important to know that some behaviors run their course no matter what you do. At other times, what starts as a normal behavior pattern jumps the track and becomes a negative habit. At age three, it is too soon know if the behavior has approached that boundary. Some tips to curb the behavior, or to proactively steer it to a more acceptable tone for you are:

Be prepared to redirect their request with a calm voice, stating,"I won't hear you when you ask that way. Try again, please"

Attempt to respond as consistently as possible. Avoid the temptation to answer in a whiny voice. Children learn from the behavior you model. If you answer in a calm and patient manner, they will eventually adopt that approach naturally.

Make an effort to determine whether the behavior escalates when the child is tired or feels insecure. If so, you can take steps to change the environment or reassure the child. He or she will find it comforting to resort to a more familiar routine, knowing what to expect next.

As the child matures, continue to teach more effective ways to communicate his or her needs.

Recommended Resources

Essa, E. (2003). *A practical guide to solving preschool behavior problems.*
Clifton Park: Thomson Delmar Learning.

QUESTIONS ABOUT HEARING FOR YOUNG CHILDREN

My son has a history of ear infections and his words are garbled. Should I be concerned?

A child who repeatedly suffers from ear infections may be at risk for impaired hearing. Sometimes the inflammation in the middle ear goes undetected, due to lack of symptoms, and a fluid-build up affects the ability to hear well. Although it is impossible to measure what damage has occurred, it is advisable to seek medical attention.

My daughter speaks very loudly, especially after she has spent time in her play group. Is she hard of hearing?

Children naturally mimic the environment they are exposed to. They find it difficult to modulate their voices on their own. Sometimes they are so excited with their play experience that they do not realize their voices have reached a loud pitch. Attempt to help her lower her voice by speaking softly to her, or ask her to whisper with you. In a few moments, she should be able to emulate a softer tone. If such repeated efforts produce no results, perhaps a visit to the family doctor is in order to rule out a build-up of fluid or wax in the ear. Or the doctor may simply reassure you that her voice matches her enthusiastic personality.

My child seems to ignore me when I speak to him. Could this be on purpose, or is it a possible hearing loss?

Both are plausible answers to your question. Have you tried standing quietly behind your child and speaking a question? Does your child only respond when you make eye contact? If you are unable to illicit a response to either types of attempts then a possible hearing impairment might exist. Finding the answers to these questions might help you decide if it is time to visit a health professional.

Sometimes my three-year-old daughter uses the wrong words, or uses the same ones repeatedly. Does she have a hearing impairment?

It is normal for a three-year-old to misuse and mispronounce words when speaking. If you have ever studied a foreign language, you will remember you were not fluent overnight. Her vocabulary has grown by at least 500–1000 words in the last year, and she is valiantly practicing this skill to the best of her ability by repeating words over and over until she can assimilate their proper usage. With that said, you should note as the months evolve that she will noticeably improve, and if you still are concerned, seek professional advice.

Helpful Website:

American Audiology Association at http://www.audiology.com

WHEN DOES THE LEARNING START?

How do you incorporate learning throughout the day?

In the activities we do, in the experiences we create, and even in the free play, your child is learning. He or she is learning to interact with peers and adults through conversation and free play. By creating simple art projects, your child is refining his or her fine motor skills. We send home all sorts of art projects that involved cutting, coloring, pasting, and otherwise controlling hands and fingers. When we play outside on the playground, your child is jumping, climbing, and learning to control large movements. In every thing we do, learning is somehow incorporated.

How does playing games teach my child?

We play a variety of simple games that incorporate gross motor skills. These help your child improve those skills and develop hand-eye coordination, balance, flexibility, and many other physical and mental skills. We are encouraging your child to be healthy and active, which starts very young. Playing games also helps teach children how to follow complex directions. Socially, your child is also learning to take turns and share. As we play more and more games, she or he will also learn teamwork.

When does my child start learning to read?

Each child begins to read at a different pace. It is important to regularly read to your child to get her or him interested in reading. Your child will not only enjoy spending time with you, but will begin to understand the function of words in print. He or she will learn the beginning steps of holding the book the correct way, understanding that the words have meaning, and, in time, will begin to recognize letters. Learning to read is a long process, and each child's experience is different.

What can I do at home to supplement what my child learns in preschool?

In addition to reading to children, it is equally as important to regularly talk with and listen to them. Ask your child about his or her day and talk about your own day. Find out what theme the children are discussing in preschool and ask your child about what he or she is learning. It is also important to encourage your child to use his imagination. Make up stories together or play pretend. Also, provide experiences for your child explore and learn. Whether you pull weeds out of the garden or take a walk in your neighborhood, any time you spend with your child is a huge benefit to his or her learning. Spending quality time with your child is one of the most important things you can do to provide encouragement to learn and grow.

Where can I find activities to do at home to help my child learn?

Parenting magazines, which also have articles on the Internet, can be a great source for finding creative ways to help your child learn.

PINK EYE

What is it?

Pink eye, or conjunctivitis, is an infection of the eye caused by either bacteria or virus.

What does it look like?

The white part of the eye becomes pink. The affected eye produces copious amounts of tears and possible cream- or green-colored discharge. The affected eye may itch. Sometimes, upon awakening from sleep, the eye may remain closed because the discharge has matted to the eye lashes.

What is the incubation period?

The incubation period is from one to three days.

How long is it contagious?

Treat the discharge from the eye as contagious until treated by a physician.

How does it spread?

Pink eye spreads by direct contact with other children. Children often pass the infection by rubbing their itching eye and then touching something or someone. The condition is spread by direct contact with the contaminated hand or item.

What is a proper plan of action?

1. Isolate the infected person
2. Notify the child's parents
3. Suggest parents seek medical supervision for treatment and medication
4. Check all other children for potential symptoms of infection
5. Sanitize toys and equipment as soon as possible and do not wait for the scheduled cleaning day
6. Review hand washing procedures
7. Post a notice on the events bulletin board

Who should be notified?

The parents of the infected child should be notified. Notify other parents and staff to watch for signs and symptoms.

When can a child resume contact with other children?

A bacterial infection is treated with antibiotics. The child may return to the day care center 24 hours after beginning treatment.

Viral conjunctivitis must be diagnosed and confirmed by a physician. Once the condition is determined not to be a bacterial infection, the child may return when feeling well enough.

Helpful Website:

American Academy of Pediatrics at http:// www.aap.org

Recommended Resources

Polly, J. A. (2000). *The internet kids & family yellow pages.* Berkely, CA: McGraw-Hill.

Rimm, S. (1996). *Dr. Dylvia Rimm's smart parenting.* New York: Crown Publishers, Inc.

VanGorp, L. (2001). *1001 Best websites for parents.* Westminister, CA: Teacher Created Materials Inc.

Index

To find your specific
State's Licensing, Rules
and Regulations go to:

http://nrc.uchsc.edu

APPENDIX

A

Forms and Templates

Organized by chapter, this appendix contains the following forms and templates for your convenience:

Classroom Cleaning Schedule
For the Week of ___
Classroom ___

#	Daily Cleaning Projects	Mon	Tue	Wed	Thr	Fri	Once-A-Week Projects	Initial	Date
1.	Mop floors						Scrub, brush & mop in corners		
2.	Clean all sinks with cleanser						Wipe off cubbies / shelves		
3.	Wipe around sinks						Wipe/disinfect bathroom walls		
4.	Clean toilets with brush in & out						Clean & disinfect all stools		
5.	Clean & disinfect water fountains						Clean outside window door		
6.	Clean inside of windows and seals						Launder small rugs		
7.	Clean inside & outside glass on doors						Organize shelves		
8.	Clean & disinfect changing table						Move furniture to vacuum and sweep		
9.	Run vacuum (carpet & rugs)						Wipe out / inside of paper trash can		
10.	Dispose of trash (replace bag!)						Wipe underneath tables & the legs		
11.	Wipe outside of all cans & lids						Wipe chair backs and legs		
12.	Clean & disinfect diaper receptacles								
13.	Wipe off tables/chairs						**Immediate Project**		
14.	Wipe off & disinfect cots						Any surface contaminated with body fluids such as blood, stool, mucous, vomit, or urine.		
15.	Reduce clutter! (Organize!)								
16.	Wipe/disinfect door handles						**Quarterly**		
17.	Clean and disinfect toys						Clean carpets		
18.									

Lead Teacher: ___

KIDEX *for* THREES
Class Book

_____
GROUP NAME

DAILY THREES SCHEDULE OUTLINE

Early Morning	
Mid Morning	
Late Morning	
Mid Day	
Early Afternoon	
Mid Afternoon	
Late Afternoon	
Early Evening	

DAILY THREES SCHEDULE DETAILS

Early Morning	
Mid Morning	
Late Morning	
Mid Day	
Early Afternoon	
Mid Afternoon	
Late Afternoon	
Early Evening	

Introduce Us to Your Three-Year-Old
(37–48 Months)

Date _____

Last Name: _____ First Name: _____ Middle: _____

Name your child is called at home: _____

Siblings: Names & Ages: _____

Favorite Play Materials: _____

Special Interests: _____

Pets: _____

What opportunities does your child have to play with others the same age? _____

_____

Eating Patterns:

    Are there any dietary concerns? _____

    Does your child feed him/herself?   Independent _____ Needs Assistance _____

    Are there any food dislikes? _____

    Are there any food allergies? _____

Sleeping Patterns:

    What time is bedtime at home? _____ Arise at? _____

    What time is nap time? _____ How long? _____

    Does your child have a special toy/blanket to nap with? _____

    How is your child prepared for rest (e.g., story time, quiet play, snack)

    _____

Eliminating Patterns:

    Toilet trained yet?   Yes _____ No _____

    If not, when do you anticipate introducing toilet training? _____

    Would you like more information? _____

    In training? _____ If trained, how long? _____

    Is independent—doesn't require help. _____

    Does your child need to be reminded? _____

    If yes, at what time intervals do you suggest? _____

    Does your child have certain words to indicate a need to eliminate? _____

    _____

Child wears:

Nap time diaper _____   Disposable training pants _____

Cloth underwear _____   Plastic pants over cloth underwear _____

Stress/Coping Patterns:

Does your child have any fears: _____ Storms _____ Separation anxiety _____

Dark _____   Animals _____   Stranger anxiety _____

Being alone _____   Other _____

How do you soothe him or her?_____

Personality Traits: shy/reserved   outgoing/curious   sensitive/frightens easily
(Circle all that apply)   very verbal   active   restless
                             cuddly   demonstrative   cautious
                             warms slowly to new people or situations

Health Patterns:

List other allergy alerts: _____

List any medications, intervals, and route (mouth, ears, eyes, etc):

_____

List any health issues or special needs: _____

_____

How often a day do you assist your child with brushing his or her teeth? _____

Is there any other information we should know in order to help us know your child better?

_____

_____

_____

_____
Parent / Guardian completing form

OFFICE USE ONLY
Start Date: _____ Full Time: _____ Part Time: S M T W T F S ½ a.m. p.m.
Group Assigned: a.m. _____ p.m. _____
Teacher(s): _____
Please keep an adjustment record yes _____ no _____ for _____ weeks.
Assign a cubby space: _____ Assign a diaper space: _____

KIDEX for Threes
Individual Monthly Profile

Month: _____ Teacher: _____

Child's Name: _____ Group: _____

Age: _____ Birth Date: _____ Allergy Alerts: _____

Parents'/Guardians' Names: _____ Start Date: _____

When Eating Uses: independent _____   needs assistance _____

Food dislikes: _____

Diapers: _____ Nap Time Diaper Only: _____ Toilet Trained: _____

Independent: _____ Needs reminding/assistance: _____ Toilet training: _____

Special Diapering Instructions (special ointments, etc.): _____

Personality Traits: shy/reserved outgoing/curious   sensitive/frightens easily
(Circle all that apply)   very verbal   active   restless
                             cuddly   demonstrative   cautious
                             warms slowly to new people or situations

Health Concerns: _____

Daily Medications: yes _____   no _____   (see med sheet for details)

Special Needs Instructions: _____

Stress/Coping Pattern: fears _____   storms _____   loudness _____   strangers _____
          dark _____   animals _____   separation anxiety _____   others _____

Special Blanket/Toy: _____ Name: _____

Average Nap Length: _____

Special Nap Instructions: _____

_____

Favorite Activities This Month: _____

Days Attending: Sun.   Mon.   Tues.   Wed.   Thurs.   Fri.   Sat.   1/2 days   Full days

Approximate Arrival Time _____ Approximate Departure Time _____

Those authorized to pick up: _____

_____

Warning: If name is not listed, consult with office and obtain permission to release child.
If you are not familiar with this person, always request I.D.

TOILET TRAINING

Child's Name:_____
Lead Teacher:_____ Date:_____

Time	Wet	B.M.	Dry	Refused	Seemed Confused	Comments
6:00 – 6:30						
6:30 – 7:00						
7:00 – 7:30						
7:30 – 8:00						
8:00 – 8:30						
8:30 – 9:00						
9:00 – 9:30						
9:30 – 10:00						
10:00 – 10:30						
10:30 – 11:00						
11:00 – 11:30						
11:30 – 12:00						
12:00 – 12:30						
12:30 – 1:00						
1:00 – 1:30						
1:30 – 2:00						
2:00 – 2:30						
2:30 – 3:00						
3:00 – 3:30						
3:30 – 4:00						
4:00 – 4:30						
4:30 – 5:00						
5:00 – 5:30						
5:30 – 6:00						
6:00 – 6:30						
6:30 – 7:00						
7:00 – 7:30						
7:30 – 8:00						

Diaper Changing Schedule

Day: _____   **Date:** _____

Child's Name	8:00 am–9:00 am			11:00 am–12:00 pm			After Nap			5:00 pm–6:00 pm			Bedtime			Wake up		
	BM	WET	DRY	BM	WET	DRY	BM	WET	DRY	BM	WET	DRY	BM	WET	DRY	BM	WET	DRY
1.																		
2.																		
3.																		
4.																		
5.																		
6.																		
7.																		
8.																		
9.																		
10.																		
11.																		
12.																		

Initial the appropriate box when diapering is completed.

PROGRAM ENROLLING APPLICATION

Child's Full Name: _____ Nickname: _____

Date of Birth: _____ Sex: _____ Home Phone: _____

Address: _____ City: _____ Zip Code: _____

Legal Guardian: _____

Mother's Name: _____Home Phone: _____

Cell Phone: _____ E-Mail: _____

Address: _____ City: _____ Zip Code: _____

Employer: _____ Work Phone: _____

Address: _____ City: _____ Zip Code: _____

Father's Name: _____Home Phone: _____

Cell Phone: _____ E-Mail: _____

Address: _____ City: _____ Zip Code: _____

Employer: _____ Work Phone: _____

IN THE EVENT YOU CANNOT BE REACHED IN AN EMERGENCY, CALL:

Name: _____ Relationship: _____ Phone: _____

Address: _____ City: _____ Zip Code: _____

Name: _____ Relationship: _____ Phone: _____

Address: _____ City: _____ Zip Code: _____

OTHER PEOPLE RESIDING WITH CHILD

Name: _____ Relationship: _____ Age: _____

Name: _____ Relationship: _____ Age: _____

Name: _____ Relationship: _____ Age: _____

PEOPLE AUTHORIZED TO REMOVE CHILD FROM THE CENTER:

Your child will not be allowed to leave the center with anyone whose name does not appear on this application, or who does not have an "authorization card" provided by you, or unless you make other arrangements with the Center's management. Positive I.D. will be required.

Name: _____ Relationship: _____

Name: _____ Relationship: _____

Name: _____ Relationship: _____

Child Will Attend: Mon - Tues - Wed - Thur - Fri - Sat - Sun

Child Will Be:Full Time or Part Time

Time Child Will Be Dropped Off (Normally): _____

Time Child Will Be Picked Up (Normally): _____

MEDICAL INFORMATION/AUTHORIZATION

Physician's Name: _____ Phone: _____

Address: _____ City: _____ Zip Code: _____

Dentist's Name: _____ Phone: _____

Address: _____ City: _____ Zip Code: _____

Allergies: _____

I agree and give consent, that in case of accident, injury, or illness of a serious nature, my child will be given medical attention/emergency care. I understand I will be contacted immediately, or as soon as possible if I am away from the numbers listed on this form.

PERMISSION TO LEAVE PREMISES

I hereby give the School/Center _____ permission to take my
                                            (name)
child on neighborhood walks.   YES _____ (INITIAL)

NO, I do not give permission at this time: _____ (INITIAL)

Parent/Guardian's Signature: _____

Parent/Guardian's Signature: _____

Date: _____

AUTHORIZED
PERSON
CARD

AUTHORIZED
PERSON
CARD

AUTHORIZED
PERSON
CARD

AUTHORIZED
PERSON
CARD

AUTHORIZED
PERSON
CARD

AUTHORIZED
PERSON
CARD

AUTHORIZED
PERSON
CARD

AUTHORIZED
PERSON
CARD

AUTHORIZED
PERSON
CARD

AUTHORIZED
PERSON
CARD

USE HEAVY CARD STOCK (FRONT OF CARD)

Name of Authorized Person

May pick up my child _____

on my behalf.

_____ _____
Parent/Guardian Signature   Date

Name of Authorized Person

May pick up my child _____

on my behalf.

_____ _____
Parent/Guardian Signature   Date

Name of Authorized Person

May pick up my child _____

on my behalf.

_____ _____
Parent/Guardian Signature   Date

Name of Authorized Person

May pick up my child _____

on my behalf.

_____ _____
Parent/Guardian Signature   Date

Name of Authorized Person

May pick up my child _____

on my behalf.

_____ _____
Parent/Guardian Signature   Date

Name of Authorized Person

May pick up my child _____

on my behalf.

_____ _____
Parent/Guardian Signature   Date

Name of Authorized Person

May pick up my child _____

on my behalf.

_____ _____
Parent/Guardian Signature   Date

Name of Authorized Person

May pick up my child _____

on my behalf.

_____ _____
Parent/Guardian Signature   Date

Name of Authorized Person

May pick up my child _____

on my behalf.

_____ _____
Parent/Guardian Signature   Date

Name of Authorized Person

May pick up my child _____

on my behalf.

_____ _____
Parent/Guardian Signature   Date

USE HEAVY CARD STOCK (BACK OF CARD)

Threes Daily Observation Checklist

Child's name: _____   Date: _____
Arrival: _____   Departure: _____

	Breakfast	Snack	Lunch	Snack	Dinner	Evening Snack
Ate Partial (Less than half)						
Ate Complete						

	Medications *	Treatments *
Time		
Time		
Time		
* see daily medication sheets for details		

Nap Times: _____   Diaper and Toilet Training Progress (See attached Sheet)
                               Yes _____   N/A _____
Comments: _____   Lead Teacher: _____
                                     Shift Time: _____
_____   Teacher: _____
                                     Shift Time: _____
_____   Teacher: _____
                                     Shift Time: _____
_____   Teacher: _____
                                     Shift Time: _____

Threes Daily Observation Checklist

Child's name: _____   Date: _____
Arrival: _____   Departure: _____

	Breakfast	Snack	Lunch	Snack	Dinner	Evening Snack
Ate Partial (Less than half)						
Ate Complete						

	Medications *	Treatments *
Time		
Time		
Time		
* see daily medication sheets for details		

Nap Times: _____   Diaper and Toilet Training Progress (See attached Sheet)
                               Yes _____   N/A _____
Comments: _____   Lead Teacher: _____
                                     Shift Time: _____
_____   Teacher: _____
                                     Shift Time: _____
_____   Teacher: _____
                                     Shift Time: _____
_____   Teacher: _____
                                     Shift Time: _____

OUR DAY

Group Name: _____

DATE _____   Day of Week _____

Early morning activities/centers: (Beginning the day during morning arrival)

_____

_____

KIDEX Fun with Language and Telling Tales : **Activities to build our vocabulary were:**

_____

Finger plays & songs we sang today were:

_____

Circle Time Concept: _____

Our morning outdoor activity was:

_____

KIDEX My Body is Wonderful: **Activities to exercise our fine and large muscles were:**

_____

Our morning project was:

_____

_____

AFTERNOON

KIDEX Exploring My World/Creating My Way: **Our creative/sensory activities were:**

_____

_____

The story we read was:

_____

Our afternoon outdoor activity was:

_____

Late afternoon activities/centers: (Ending the day during departures)

_____

_____

_____

Extra activities today were:

_____

EATING PATTERNS

Week of _____

Classroom	Monday					Tuesday					Wednesday					Thursday					Friday					Saturday					Sunday				
Child's Name	Breakfast	Snack	Lunch	Snack	Dinner	Breakfast	Snack	Lunch	Snack	Dinner	Breakfast	Snack	Lunch	Snack	Dinner	Breakfast	Snack	Lunch	Snack	Dinner	Breakfast	Snack	Lunch	Snack	Dinner	Breakfast	Snack	Lunch	Snack	Dinner	Breakfast	Snack	Lunch	Snack	Dinner

P = Ate Partial (less than half)   C = Complete

Rest Time

Classroom _____

Week of _____

Name	Monday			Tuesday			Wednesday			Thursday			Friday			Saturday			Sunday		
	Asleep	Awake	Reading	Asleep	Awake	Reading	Asleep	Awake	Reading	Asleep	Awake	Reading	Asleep	Awake	Reading	Asleep	Awake	Reading	Asleep	Awake	Reading

Child Transitioning Report

Name _____ Teacher _____

Date of Report _____ Teacher _____

Day 1 2 3 4 5 6 7 8 9 10 11 12 13 14 15

	NOT YET	SOME	FREQUENTLY
Played with learning materials	_____	_____	_____
Participated in activities	_____	_____	_____
Played with the children	_____	_____	_____

Appetite	COMPLETE	PARTIAL (Less than half)
Breakfast appetite	_____	_____
AM snack appetite	_____	_____
Lunch appetite	_____	_____
PM snack appetite	_____	_____
Dinner appetite	_____	_____

Rest Time

Indicate time   From _____ To _____

Bowel & bladder pattern (See diaper changing sheet if applicable)

Overall day

Great! _____   *Seemed comfortable with new environment*

Fair   _____   *Adjustments to the new group and environment will improve as your child grows accustomed to the new environment*

Staff Comments:_____

Parent's Comments or Questions (If any): _____

Use for 1-3 weeks until the new child feels comfortable with the group.

Posted Hand Washing Procedures

1	Turn on warm water* and adjust to comfortable temperature.	2	Wet hands and apply soap.	3	Wash vigorously for approximately 15–20 seconds.
4	Dry hands with paper towel.	5	Turn off faucet with paper towel.	6	Dispose of paper towel in a lidded trash receptacle with a plastic liner.

Use hand washing procedures for staff and children

- before and after preparing bottles or serving food.
- before and after diapering or toileting.
- before and after administering first aid.
- before and after giving medication.
- before working with the children and at the end of the day.
- before leaving the classroom for a break.
- after wiping nose discharge, coughing, or sneezing.
- before and after playing in the sand and water table.
- after playing with pets.
- after playing outdoors.

*Some states require cold water for children's hand washing sinks.
 Check your state for specific guidelines.

Daily Medications

Child's Name	RX Number & Type of Medication	Amount & Route Administered	Date	Time	Given By:	
					First Name	Last Name

Medical Authorization
for Nonprescription Medication*

Name of Child: _____   Date: _____

The staff is authorized to dispense the following medications as ordered by your physician and directed by the parents/guardian.

Please indicate specific medication, route it is to be given, dosage, and frequency.

Type	Medication	Route	Dosage	Frequency
Nonaspirin Preparation				
Aspirin Preparation				
Cough Preparation				
Decongestant				
Skin Ointment				
Diaper Wipes				
Sunscreen				

_____   _____   _____
Print Name of Physician   Signature of Physician   Phone Number

_____
Parent/Guardian Signature

Complete this form on admission and update annually. Store medical authorizations in an index box and place in or near locked cabinet for quick referencing.

SUGGESTED ILLNESS

Child's name: _____   Date: _____

SYMPTOMS ARE:

_____   Body Temperature (under arm, add 1 degree)

_____   Vomiting

_____   Diarrhea

_____   Exhibiting signs of a communicable illness

_____   Skin condition requiring further treatment

Other: _____

Report initiated by: _____

Were parents notified? Yes _____ No _____ By whom? _____

Time parents notified: 1st Attempt _____

                           _____
                           Which Parent Notified

                           2nd Attempt _____

                           _____
                           Which Parent Notified

                           3rd Attempt _____

                           _____
                           Which Parent Notified

Time child departed: _____

Director's signature: _____

Children exhibiting a temperature that exceeds 100°F, symptoms of vomiting (1–3 forceful rushes), diarrhea (defined as watery, mucous, foul-smelling bowel movement) or an unrecognized rash shall not return to group care for a minimum of 24 hours after treatment or before symptoms subside.

1. Office Copy   2. Parent/Guardian Copy

Illness Tracking Reports

Name of Child	Date	Time Called	Type of Illness	Person Reporting Illness	Director Notified	Report Filed	Parent Notified	Time Left

Head Lice Checklist

Group Name: _____

Name	Sunday	Monday	Tuesday	Wednesday	Thursday	Friday	Saturday

C = Clear   **A = Absent**   **P = Possible**

(**Reminder**:   *Please check weekly on different days of the week.*)

SUGGESTED FIRST AID DIRECTIVES

CHOKING

(Conscious) - Stand or kneel behind child with your arms around his waist and make a fist. Place thumb side of fist in the middle of abdomen just above the navel. With moderate pressure, use your other hand to press fist into child's abdomen with a quick, upward thrust. Keep your elbows out and away from child. Repeat thrusts until obstruction is cleared or child begins to cough or becomes unconscious.

(Unconscious) - Position child on his back. Just above navel, place heel of one hand on the midline of abdomen with the other hand placed on top of the first. Using moderate pressure, press into abdomen with a quick, upward thrust. Open airway by tilting head back and lifting chin. **If you can see the object**, do a finger sweep. Slide finger down inside of cheek to base of tongue, sweep object out but be careful not to push the object deeper into the throat. Repeat above until obstruction is removed or child begins coughing. If child does not resume breathing, proceed with artificial respiration (see below).

Infants - Support infant's head and neck. Turn infant face down on your forearm. Lower your forearm onto your thigh. Give four (4) back blows forcefully between infant's shoulder blades with heel of hand. Turn infant onto back. Place middle and index fingers on breastbone between nipple line and end of breastbone. Quickly compress breastbone one-half to one inch with each thrust. Repeat backblows and chest thrusts until object is coughed up, infant starts to cry, cough, and breathe, or medical personnel arrives and takes over.

POISONING

Call Poison Control Center (1-800-382-9097) immediately! Have the poison container handy for reference when talking to the center. Do not induce vomiting unless instructed to do so by a health professional. Check the child's airway, breathing, and circulation.

HEMORRHAGING

Use a protective barrier between you and the child (gloves). Then, with a clean pad, apply firm continuous pressure to the bleeding site for five minutes. Do not move/change pads, but you may place additional pads on top of the original one. If bleeding persists, call the doctor or ambulance Open wounds may require a tetanus shot.

SEIZURE

Clear the area around the child of hard or sharp objects. Loosen tight clothing around the neck. Do not restrain the child. Do not force fingers or objects into the child's mouth. After the seizure is over and if the child is not experiencing breathing difficulties, lay him/her on his/her side until he/she regains consciousness or until he/she can be seen by emergency medical personnel. After the seizure, allow the child to rest. Notify parents immediately. If child is experiencing breathing difficulty, or if seizure is lasting longer than 15 minutes, call an ambulance at once.

ARTIFICIAL RESPIRATION *(Rescue Breathing)*

Position child on the back; if not breathing, open airway by gently tilting the head back and lifting chin. Look, listen, and feel for breathing. If still not breathing, keep head tilted back and pinch nose shut. Give two full breaths and then one regular breath every 4 seconds thereafter. Continue for one minute; then look, listen, and feel for the return of breathing. Continue rescue breathing until medical help arrives or breathing resumes.

If using one-way pulmonary resuscitation device, be sure your mouth and child's mouth are sealed around the device.

(Modification for infants only)   Proceed as above, but place your mouth over nose and mouth of the infant. Give light puffs every 3 seconds.

SHOCK

If skin is cold and clammy, as well as face pale or child has nausea or vomiting, or shallow breathing, call for emergency help. Keep the child lying down. Elevate the feet. If there are head/chest injuries, raise the head and shoulders only.

Accident/Incident

Child's Name: _____

Date of accident/injury: _____ Time: _____

Brief description of accident/injury: _____

_____

_____

Was first aid given? _____ If so, describe: _____

_____

Was blood present in accident? _____ How much? _____

Were Universal Precautions employed? _____

Was medical intervention required?* _____ If yes, describe: _____

_____

Person initiating this report: _____ Witness: _____

Name of parent contacted: _____ Time contacted: _____

Director's signature: _____

*In some states it is required to file a copy of this report with the child care licensing department if medical intervention is required.

Accident/Incident Tracking Reports

Name of Child	Date	Time	Type of Accident	Person Reporting Accident	Director Notified	Report Filed	Parent Notified	Time Called

FIELD TRIP CHECKLIST

Destination:_____ Departure Time:_____ Return Time:_____

Date: _____ Class: _____ Lead Teacher: _____

Consult annual field trip schedule the 1st week of each month.

TO MAKE

___ RSVP List
___ Fill attendance sheet
___ Name Tags/ID Name/Center ID Tags
___ Emergency information and medical authorization for all children and staff attending field trip
___ Several changes of clothing, hand wipes, tissues, paper towels, etc. are packed and assigned to a staff member.
___ First aid kit for bus/van

GIVE TO STAFF

___ Name tags
___ Attendance sheet (night before)
___ Time of departure & arrival
___ Time to start preparing to leave
___ Money for extra tickets or expenses (if necessary)
___ Agenda of trip (for long trips)

STAFF DUTIES

___ Know what duties they are to perform on trip
___ Have children tagged and ready to leave at designated time
___ Review trip rules with children
___ If lunch is to be taken, make sure it is packed on bus/van

___ **Take Attendance sheet**
  1st time: Attendance in class
  2nd time: Attendance on bus before field trip
  3rd time: Planned attendance check during field trip
  4th time: Gathered on van/bus before departure
  5th time: Attendance in class after return
___ Remind children to use the restroom before departure
___ Take updated attendance - leave copy at the office

USING VAN/BUS

___ Does it have gas?
___ Does it have enough seats to accommodate all passengers? If not, who is responsible for transporting extra volunteers and staff?
___ Who will drive the van/bus?

FOOD

___ Water cooler packed?
___ Do children and adults need a sack lunch?
    ___ How many?
    ___ Has cook been notified?
___ Do snacks or lunch need to be served at a different time?
___ Has cook been notified?

NOTICES TO BE COMPLETED

___ Post a note about the field trip 1 month ahead of time on the current event bulletin board
___ Collect written permission from parents

MISCELLANEOUS

___ One person should be responsible for the attendance form throughout the entire field trip
___ Take children's emergency/health information on bus/van
___ Will extra staff or volunteers be needed?
    ___ Who?
    ___ How many?
___ If trip is on an extra activity day (dance, piano, etc.), has teacher of the activity been notified?
___ Does the class need to be rescheduled?
___ What are the times & places?
___ Place agenda in writing and give to staff & volunteers the day before
___ Collect ID tags after trip
___ Turn in receipts/check stubs
___ Turn in completed attendance sheet. This form should be filed for reference in case the State requests them
___ Never leave children unsupervised
___ Take first aid kit for bus/van
___ Take cell phone for emergencies

FIELD TRIP INFORMATION SHEET

Lead Teacher: _____ Date of Field Trip: _____

Estimated Hours: _____

Field Trip Destination: _____

Address: _____

Directions for Van/Bus Driver: _____

_____

_____

Phone: _____ Contact Person: _____ Van/Bus Driver: _____

Field Trip Purpose: _____

Actual Time Left: _____ Actual Time Returned: _____ Fee Per Child: _____

Staff Attending: _____ Parents' Attending: _____

_____ _____

_____ _____

_____ _____

1. Attendance in class **2**. Attendance on bus before field trip **3**. Planned attendance check during field trip
4. Gathered on van/bus before departure **5**. Attendance in class after return

	Children Attending	**1**	**2**	**3**	**4**	**5**	**Parent's Permission** (optional)
1							
2							
3							
4							
5							
6							
7							
8							
9							
10							
11							
12							
13							
14							
15							
16							
17							
18							
19							
20							

Emergency Contacts: *Post Near Every Telephone*

Your Facility Address: _____

_____

Nearest Main Intersection: _____

Your Facility Phone Number: _____

Contact	Phone Number
Operator	
Emergency	
Fire	
Police	
Consulting Dentist	
Poison Control	
Local Hospital Emergency Dept	
Other	
Other	

Emergency Evacuation Plan

Draw first choice escape route; draw second choice escape route

Center's Address: _____

Nearest Main Intersection: _____

Center's Phone Number: _____

In Case of Fire Call: _____

In Case of Bomb Threat Call: _____

In Case of Gas Leak Call: _____

Fire Extinguisher Expires Date: _____

Emergency Bag and Blanket Are Located: _____

Stretch the evacuation rope out on the floor. Have each child grab a knot and hold tight. Account for all children in attendance. If the door is cool, open door slowly, make sure fire or smoke isn't blocking your escape route. If your escape is blocked, close the door and use alternative escape route. Smoke and heat rise. Be prepared to crawl where the air is clearer and cooler near the floor. Move as far from the building as possible. In case of a real fire, do not reenter the building until it is cleared by the proper authorities.

How to create an emergency evacuation rope:

Create an emergency evacuation rope by using a rope long enough for 5-7 children. Tie a knot every 12" for them to hold onto and guide them to a safe area.

When the rope is not in use, place it on a hook out of reach to avoid a potential strangulation accident.

12"   12"   12"   12"   12"   12"   12"

Hurricane Emergency Instructions

Hurricane/Tropical Storm Watch: indicates conditions are possible in the specified area within 36 hours.

Hurricane/Tropical Storm Warning: conditions are expected within 24 hours.

Send the children home.
Learn your specific evacuation route.
Secure your facility.
Close storm shutters.
Turn utilities off at main valves if instructed by authorities.
Take emergency phone numbers with you.

Your evacuation route: _____

_____

_____

Tornado Emergency Instructions

Your county or region is: _____

Tornado Watch: A tornado is possible. Remain alert for approaching storms. Tune your portable (battery-operated) radio to a local weather station.

Tornado Warning: A tornado has been sighted. Activate your emergency shelter plan immediately.

Grab your emergency bag and blanket. They are located: _____

_____

For three-year-olds — Stretch the evacuation rope out on the floor. Evacuation rope is located:
_____
Have each child grab a knot and hold on tight. Account for all children in attendance. Move children calmly and quickly to an interior room or hallway.
Your best location is: _____

_____

_____

_____

_____

_____

Cover the children with heavy blankets or cushions, if available, in case of flying glass or debris.

Avoid windows, doors, outside walls, and corners of rooms.

Earthquake Emergency Instructions

Prior to earthquakes:
- Brace high and top-heavy objects.
- Fasten cubbies, lockers, toy shelves to the wall.
- Anchor overhead lighting fixtures.
- Install flexible pipe fitting to avoid gas or water leaks.
- Know when and how to shut off electricity, gas, and water at main switches and valves.
- Locate safe spots in the room to protect yourself from dropping debris such as under a sturdy table or crib.

Your safest location is: _____

The shutoff for gas is located: _____

The water main is located: _____

Your emergency bag is located: _____

During an earthquake:

- Stay inside until shaking stops and it is safe to go outside.
- Move the children to your safe location (on an inside wall) or under sturdy table.
- Describe where: _____

_____

_____

_____

- Place a heavy blanket over the children to protect them from falling debris.
- If you are on the playground, move away from the building.

When the shaking stops be prepared for aftershocks. Check for injuries and administer first aid as indicated. Use flashlights if electricity is out. DO NOT light candles or matches in case of gas leakage.

Tornado/Earthquake Drill Log

Date	Time of Drill	Time Needed to Seek Cover	Comments	Full Name of Person in Charge

Building Evacuation Log

Date	Time of Drill	Evacuation Time	Comments	Full Name of Person in Charge

Spread The Word

Threes Weekly Lesson Plans

Stage of Play Development: Emerging from parallel play into symbolic and early stages of cooperative play

Week of: _____
Group Name: _____
Theme: _____
Lead Teacher: _____

Activities	Sun	Mon	Tues	Wed	Thurs	Fri	Sat
Concept							
Circle Time (Whole Group)							
Language Skills							
KIDEX *Fun with Language & Telling Tales* Activities							
Songs/Finger Plays							
Reading/Stories (Flannel Board/ Vocabulary/ Puppets)							
KIDEX: *Exploring Our World* Activities							
Cognitive/Sensory/Math/ Science Centers							
KIDEX: *Creating My Way* Activities / Arts Exploration/ Crafts							
Dramatic Play Center							
KIDEX: *My Body Is Wonderful* Activities — Large Muscle & Music Movement							
Small Muscle Movement							

Learning Centers

Housekeeping / Dramatic Play / Sensory
Science / Fine Motor / Art / Water & Sand Table
Math / Active Play / Music Movement / Toys
Library / Music / Listening / Blocks / Computer

Self-Help Skills / Social Skills

37-48 Months—Integrate and encourage the development of skills during this 12-month span

Follows directions most of the time
Helps with clean up
Verbal skills building
Basic manners (please & thank you)
Respects others space & property
Basic self-control skills
Shares most of the time

Feeds self independently
Proper hygiene (toilet flushing, hand washing, tooth brushing)
Manages own clothing (except small buttons)

Refining body movements
Body / Self awareness
Safety awareness
Building imagination
Converses with peers
Follows class rules
Cooperates with peers

3 - 3 1/2 Years

37 – 42 Months

DEVELOPMENTAL MILESTONES

THREES CAN:

_____SPEAK IN 4 – 6 WORD SENTENCES

_____FOLLOW SIMPLE DIRECTIONS MOST OF THE TIME

_____NAME BASIC COLORS (RED, BLUE, GREEN, ORANGE)

_____SORT OBJECTS INTO TWO CATEGORIES (BIG/SMALL, RED/BLUE)

_____COMPLETE: 6 – 7 PIECE PUZZLES

_____BEGIN TO PARTICIPATE IN GROUP ACTIVITIES

_____WALK FORWARD AND BACKWARD ON A LINE

_____RIDE A TRICYCLE

_____MAKE A BALL OUT OF CLAY

_____UNDERSTAND SIMPLE GAMES

_____ROLL A LARGE BALL AT A TARGET

_____CLIMB UP AND DOWN STAIRS UNASSISTED

_____STRING LARGE BEADS (4-5 BEADS)

_____DRESS AND UNDRESS INDEPENDENTLY (NEEDS HELP WITH SMALL BUTTONS OR LACES)

_____ZIP AND UNZIP

_____WASH AND DRY HANDS INDEPENDENTLY

_____STACK 5 – 10 BLOCKS

_____NAME BASIC BODY PARTS

_____PAINT WITH A LARGE BRUSH

_____USE PLEASE AND THANK YOU

_____HELP WITH CLEAN UP

_____USE TOILET INDEPENDENTLY

_____WILLING TO SHARE SOMETIMES

_____PAIR OBJECTS THAT ARE RELATED

> *Important Note: children will develop at similar rates but each in a unique pattern. If you find a child is not exhibiting the majority of characteristics listed, there could be many plausible reasons ranging from premature birth to a more reserved and cautious personality. This list is a broad overview and not inclusive of all developmental milestones three-year-olds experience.*

Y = YES	S = SOMETIMES	N = NOT YET

Child's Name: _____ Teacher: _____

Date Initiated: _____ Date Completed: _____

3 1/2 - 4 Years

43 – 48 Months
DEVELOPMENTAL MILESTONES

THREES CAN:

_____USE PRONOUNS CORRECTLY (HE, SHE, IT, HER)

_____BEGIN TO UNDERSTAND TIME CONCEPTS (DAY/NIGHT)

_____CATCH A LARGE BALL

_____USE FINGER WITH CONTROL TO PAINT OR PASTE

_____BEGIN CUTTING IN A LINE

_____NAME BASIC SHAPES (CIRCLE, SQUARE, TRIANGLE)

_____COUNT 3 – 5 OBJECTS

_____KICK A BALL IN MOTION

_____HOLD CRAYON WITH FINGERS NOT FIST

_____LISTEN TO SHORT STORIES OR BOOKS (7 – 9 MINUTES)

_____THROW A BALL OVERHAND ACCURATELY

_____LACE STRING IN SHOES OR A SEQUENCE OF HOLES

_____UNDERSTAND OPPOSITES (HOT/COLD, ON/OFF)

_____ACT OUT SIMPLE STORIES

_____DRAW LINES (HORIZONTAL, VERTICAL)

_____UNDERSTAND THAT PEOPLE ARE ALIKE AND DIFFERENT

_____POUR LIQUID FROM ONE CONTAINER TO ANOTHER

_____SCREW AND UNSCREW LIDS, TOYS, ETC.

_____USE ADJECTIVES TO DESCRIBE

_____MEMORIZE AND RECITE SHORT NURSERY RHYMES OR SONGS

_____ENGAGE IN IMAGINATIVE PLAY

_____SHOW CONCERN FOR PEERS

_____PLAY WITH OTHER CHILDREN COOPERATIVELY

> *Important Note: children will develop at similar rates but each in a unique pattern. If you find a child is not exhibiting the majority of characteristics listed, there could be many plausible reasons ranging from premature birth to a more reserved and cautious personality. This list is a broad overview and not inclusive of all developmental milestones three-year-olds experience.*

Y = YES	S = SOMETIMES	N = NOT YET

Child's Name: _____ Teacher: _____

Date Initiated: _____ Date Completed: _____

3 - 3 1/2 Years Activities

Telling Tales — Simple Picture Books — Language Activities

Category 1

- Create color books. Before beginning the project, have several pictures of different colored items cut out for the children to sort. Have a color word on paper and allow the children to paste pictures to the correct paper. Put the pages together to create the book.

- Share simple picture books with the children that show different body parts. Have the children point to his/her own body parts as you read the story. (e.g. *Can you find your knee?*)

- Read a variety of simple Dr. Seuss books. The children will enjoy the rhythm and rhyme of the books. *In a People House* can give them a chance to name objects and find them around the room. Other books allow the children opportunities to "fill in" rhyming words.

- Create a "How to" book on washing hands. Discuss and practice washing hands. Discuss and practice washing hands the correct way, then have the children help write a book about it. You can take pictures of the children at each step to help illustrate it. You could do this with many multi-step procedures you may have in your room.

- Provide books that only have pictures and encourage the children to create their own story about the characters. Have some stories the children know and don't know, so they can recall stories or create their own stories.

- Read favorite books over and over again to familiarize the children with the language and characters.

- Read familiar stories, like *Goldilocks and the Three Bears* or *The Gingerbread Man*, and let the children use a felt board and felt characters to act out the stories.

- Make a book of fabric for the children. Be sure to include a variety of fabrics with different colors and textures. Ask them to describe the fabrics.

- Read familiar books and change words to silly words and allow them to correct you. When rereading a *Clifford: The Big Red Dog* book, call the dog "Georgie" or some other name.

- Share stories that are about sharing and playing with other children.

- Create books that go along with your theme. If your theme is the snow, have the children cut out pictures of things that you can do in the snow. Have them paste the pictures on paper. You write "I can _____" on each page, filling in the blank with what is being done in the picture. (e.g. sled, ice skate, ski, make a snow angel, etc.)

- Provide a variety of books that the children can connect with. If you live near the ocean, provide books about the ocean and ocean animals for the children to look at. If you live in a busy city, then make sure you have books with pictures of your own city or any big city.

- Read books that have nursery rhymes or songs. If the children know the rhyme or song, then they can read with you.

- Read *The Very Hungry Caterpillar* and create a book about the very hungry children in your room. Have them each draw or cut and paste a picture of their favorite food. Put the pages together and add a hole or "bite" in each page.

Child's Name: _____   Teacher: _____   Date Initiated: _____   Date Completed: _____

Activities 3 – 3 ½ Years Continued

Fun With Language Activities

- Sing, sing, and sing! Teach the children simple songs or rhymes that you can sing over and over again. You may want to sing a morning song to start the day and a good-bye song to end the day.
- Share pictures of different people or faces and have the children describe how they feel, what they are wearing, what they are doing, etc.
- Provide opportunities to learn opposites. Have different kind of food available to try and describe. (e.g. The soup is hot; the juice is cold. Carrots are hard; marshmallows are soft.) Also demonstrate opposites or have the children "find" opposites. (The cup is full/empty. The lights are on/off.)
- Plan experiences for the children to participate in and then discuss. Recall what they saw, did, ate, etc. Go on field trips, walks outside, or little indoor adventures.
- Encourage them to use their imagination as well. Share or create stories about imaginary experiences. Pretend you are searching for whales in your imaginary boat or submarine.
- Discuss favorite stories and characters. Describe them together.
- Be positive about pronunciation errors. Encourage them to continue thinking and to try new words and ways to say something.
- Play copycat games where the children imitate letter sounds or silly sounds that you make.
- Ask questions about their day. Did you like playing outside? What was your favorite thing you did outside?
- If you are given short or one-word answers, ask more open-ended questions to encourage more communication.
- Show pictures of two related items and ask what the differences and similarities are between the two. (e.g. hold up a picture of a green motorcycle and a green truck)
- Go on a hunt of the unknown. Have a child find something outside, in the room, or somewhere else that they don't know what it is called. Describe it together and tell the child what it is called.
- Ask questions about things they have done before or places they have gone before. Try to help them recall as much information as they can.
- Place a favorite toy or object around the room. Encourage the children to tell you where it is located. (e.g. The truck is under the table. The truck is next to or beside the chair.)
- Sing the ABC song to get them acquainted with the letters.

Category 2

Child's Name: _____ Teacher: _____ Date Initiated: _____ Date Completed: _____

Activities 3 – 3 ½ Years Continued

My Body Is Wonderful — Large & Small Muscle Activities

	• Provide a variety of riding toys for the children to use in a large area. Create a track or obstacle course for the children to steer through. Have children role play police officers, parking attendants, etc.
	• Read stories or discuss different animals, then have the children use clay or play dough to mold the characters and then recreate the story.
	• Play simple follow the leader games and let the children lead at times. Encourage jumping, skipping, hopping, rolling, etc.
	• Set up small carnival-like games that give each child opportunities to throw a bean bag or ball at target, roll the ball to knock down the pins, etc.
	• Have the children work on fine motor skills in centers, such as stringing large beads, zipping, buttoning, snapping, lacing shoes, etc.
Category **3**	• Lead the children in different motions to songs. You can jump to the music, clap, stomp, or do any other large movements. Make up motions to songs and teach the children. (e.g. Touch your toes, pinch your nose, etc.)
	• Give children streamers or ribbons to hold onto and have them dance to music.
	• Provide a small wagon for outdoor play. Bring balls or outside toys and have them move the items from one place to another. They must fill up the wagon and carefully roll it to a new place and unload it.
	• Use a metal cookie sheet and magnets. Allow the children to move the magnets around. You can cut out different body parts (head, body, legs, arms, feet, hands), stick them to magnetic table and have the children "build" a body.
	• Fill a large container with small items, such as keys, large bolts, and large marbles. Have the children sort the items into smaller containers
	• Lead the children in simple exercises (touch your toes, reach for the sky, jump up and down, etc.) This is a good way to start the day and get those muscles working.
	• When walking outside or to another room, have them tip toe like mice or walk sideways.
	• Make a cutting pool. Place all sorts of materials that children can cut (varieties of paper, yarn, etc.) in a small wading pool. Have a bucket of scissors in the pool. Invite the children to cut in the pool. The cut materials can be used in future crafts.
	• Line up several small hula-hoops and have the children jump from hoop to hoop.
	• Provide a small teeter-totter on the playground. Show the children how to use it, and then let them push themselves up and down.

Child's Name: _____ Teacher: _____ Date Initiated: _____ Date Completed: _____

Activities 3 – 3 ½ Years Continued

Creating My Way — Creative Exploration

- Create simple cut and paste activities for the children to complete. Provide scissors to cut out pictures of things that make the child happy and paste them to the big smiley face page. Cut out different size circles and paste together the world's silliest snowman.

- Marble painting. Drop marbles in paint, place a piece of paper in a box with a lid, spoon the paint-covered marbles in the box, put the lid on tightly, and let the child shake it up. (You may want to tape the lid down just in case.)

- Fill various cups with colored water. Place the cups of water in the water table and allow them to explore pouring the water on paper, mixing the colors, etc. Add soap to make it a little more fun with bubbles.

- Provide large paper and large paintbrushes for the children to paint pictures. Make sure the paint is washable and the children wear smocks. It can get messy!

- To help children gain more fine motor control, provide coloring pages of shapes and non-detailed pictures of animals for them to practice "coloring in the lines". Because creativity is limited by this activity, encourage them to use their imagination (e.g. purple dogs, orange grass, etc.)

- Paint with nature. Collect leaves, twigs, flowers, and other items to paint or print with.

- Have them practice tracing straight, curvy, and zigzag lines.

- Let them paint objects other than paper, such as pieces of wood, rocks, sticks, etc.

- Make a picture frame and let the children decorate it. You can make a square out of tongue depressors or cut a frame out of cardboard. Once the frame is made, let the children paste shells, feathers, buttons, etc. onto the frames.

- Let them paint with their feet. This is an outdoor activity and make sure they have shorts on or their pants are rolled up. Put washable paint in a shallow tray and have one child at a time step in the paint. Make sure a long sheet of butcher paper is right next to the tray and have them walk, hop, or tip toe on the paper. Be sure to have a bucket of water to wash their feet off nearby.

- Finger paint with the primary colors (red, yellow, blue). Give them two colors at a time so they can discover what happens when they mix the colors.

- Add flour or corn starch to paint so they can make bumpy paintings.

- Make wet chalk drawings. Give them dark construction paper, chalk, and a small cup of water. Have them dip the chalk into the water and then draw on the paper.

- Create paper plate masks. Allow them to decorate a paper plate with different materials. You will need to cut the eyeholes for them and glue a tongue depressor to the bottom of the plate. Then they have a mask on a stick.

- Have the children try to tear different shapes out of paper. Paste the shapes on paper to create a torn shape collage.

Category 4

Child's Name: _____ Teacher: _____ Date Initiated: _____ Date Completed: _____

Activities 3 – 3 ½ Years Continued

Exploring Our World — Activities to Explore Cognitive, Pre-Math, Sensory and Science

Category	
5	• Create a small garden space for the group. Have the children dig holes and plant seeds that they can tend to and watch grow. If there is no space for a garden, you can grow seeds in cups or plastic bags (place a folded, wet paper towel and a lima bean seed in a bag and watch the seed grow)
• Go on a nature hunt to find different shapes and textures. It can be made into a scavenger hunt as well. (e.g. find something smaller than your hand, find a green leaf, find something round.)
• Have the children help you count the class when you line up to go outside, count objects you get out, etc.
• Have the children sort pictures of people doing activities into different categories, such as things you do at night and things you do in the day.
• Provide the children with blocks and toy cars. Encourage them to build roads or a city to "drive" the cars around on.
• Make popsicles. Have the children help make fruit juice and pour it into small cups. Set a popsicle stick in the cup, so you have something to hold on to. You can keep checking on the popsicles to see how long it takes them to freeze. Then enjoy!
• Provide manipulatives for the children to explore and sort, such as beans, small jars, beads, etc.
• Use masking tape on the floor to create large shapes. Have the children walk along to tape that forms the shapes. Ask the name of the shape before a child walks it.
• Make a bubble solution, then blow the bubbles and watch the wind blow the bubbles around.
• Talk about the weather. Is it cloudy, rainy, or sunny?
• Let children play with the lights out (make sure there is a little light so they are not scared). Give each child a flashlight and allow them to experiment with shadows.
• Go on a color hunt around the room or outside.
• Challenge them to stack small cube blocks as high as they can.
• Mix colored water and oil, pour it in a clear plastic bottle, seal it tightly, and then let the children shake it up and see what happens. Add small beads or sequins to make it more exciting.
• Make sun prints. Go on a hunt for small items in nature, such as twigs, flowers, leaves, and rocks. On a sunny day place these nature items of sheets of construction paper. Leave it sitting where it won't be disturbed. If you take the items off several hours later, there will be a print where the items were placed on the paper.

Child's Name: _____   Teacher: _____   Date Initiated: _____   Date Completed: _____

3 1/2 - 4 Years Activities

Telling Tales — Simple Picture Books – Language Activities

Category **1**	• Go on a treasure hunt for rhyming words. You will need to lead them to words, such as *look at Sammie's pretty hair, hmm...let's see if we can find something in the room that sounds like hair? There is the wall, a table, a chair...*The children will figure the rhyming words out and as you find objects that rhyme, take a Polaroid or digital picture. Label each picture and put them together to form a book of rhyming words.
	• Create a book of class creations. It could be a collection of photos of block creations or any artistic creations they made in class. Label the pictures and bind them together to form a book. Or you could put pages that the children colored together to make a book of artwork.
	• Provide books about people in the community, jobs, etc. that will foster dramatic play. (e.g. If you read a book about a doctor visit, then you can turn the dramatic play area into a hospital.)
	• Make finger puppets or regular puppets and have the children act out the stories as you read or recreate the stories later.
	• Create a simple repeated line book, such as *The bear is blue. The bear is yellow.* Pointing to the words as you read helps the children see a connection between the text and the picture - the letters say something, they have a meaning.
	• When getting ready to read a book, hold the book the wrong way. Say, "I'm ready to read this book." Let the children correct you and tell you how you are supposed to hold the book.
	• Read *Something is Going to Happen!* by Charlotte Zolotow. Give each child a picture of a front door open on a house. Have the children draw what they wish to see outside their front door. Put these pages together to make a class book.
	• Find books that have at least two characters in the pictures. Have the students become the "sound track" of the book. Have them share what they think the characters are saying to each other.
	• When reading a book, create voices for the different characters. The children will love to try and imitate your voices.
	• Throughout the year let the children draw pictures of whatever they want and then have them tell you what it is a picture of. Write what they say at the bottom of the page. Save several of these pieces, and then put them together to make an art book that the child can share with her parents at the end of the year.
	• Have the children create a book of who lives in their home. Give them a page shaped like a house for each member of their family (don't forget pets!) and have them draw each person or animal. Write their names (e.g. mom, dad, Sam, Lana, and Goldie) on the pages for the child.
	• Read books that require responses from the children, such as a train noise or a dog bark. This will keep them involved. They have to be good listeners so they don't miss the chance to make the noise.
	• Share a variety of books about one subject and have them compare the stories and characters. (e.g. If you are talking about kangaroos, you can read *Kangaroo* by Caroline Arnold, *Noel the Coward* by Robert Kraus, and *Katy-No-Pocket* by Emmy Payne.)
	• Find books that will help the children kick bad habits (e.g. thumb sucking) or teach them good habits (e.g. covering your mouth when you sneeze).
	• Share books with numbers in them, so the children can begin to recognize numerals.

Child's Name: _____   Teacher: _____   Date Initiated: _____   Date Completed: _____

Activities 3 ½ – 4 Years Continued

Fun With Language Activities

	• Take a short book with a simple plot apart and laminate the pages (or you can make your own short story). Have the children put the pages in the correct sequence.
	• Model conversation and encourage the children to have conversations together.
	• Start to introduce sounds that are made at the beginning of words. *Popcorn starts with the "p" sound, what else starts with that sound?* Hunt around the room or outside for ideas.
	• Encourage the children to use "please" and "thank you" throughout the day. Be sure to set an example.
	• They love to ask who, what, when, and where questions at this age. Answer the questions or explore together to find the answers.
	• Teach them short tongue twisters. They love to try and say the silly sentences. (e.g. Susie sells seashells at the seashore.)
Category **2**	• Play "I Spy" a little differently by giving clues about an object or person. Use descriptive words and talk about words you use that they may not know.
	• Discuss what happened today, earlier today, or yesterday; model the appropriate language to use when you describe something that already happened.
	• Sing songs that give directions. Think of what you want them to do and you can sing it to any tune that you know. If it is something you will say over and over again, try to keep it the same. (e.g. Sing "Put you coat away and sit in a circle" in the same tune every time you come inside from playing.)
	• Teach them how to use soft voices, medium (inside) voices, and loud (outside) voices. Discuss when you would use each one.
	• Each day, draw a mystery word from a box. Each time the children hear the word have them to show silent applause (raise hands straight up in the air and wiggle your fingers). This is a listening activity that lasts the whole day. You can also introduce new words.
	• Encourage parents to ask their child about her day. They can even write it down in a journal and read it back to the child occasionally. It is a fun way to keep parents involved and informed.
	• Use a box to teach placement and opposite words. (e.g. top/bottom, inside/outside, front/back, etc.)
	• Discuss feelings. Encourage them to express their emotions in words. (e.g. How does it feel when someone takes your toy that you are playing with?)
	• A game you can play to get children to use more descriptive words, have a child reach into a bag to feel a mystery object. That child has to describe what the object feels like to the rest of the children.

Child's Name: _____   Teacher: _____   Date Initiated: _____   Date Completed: _____

Activities 3 ½ - 4 Years Continued

My Body Is Wonderful — Large & Small Muscle Activities

- Play favorite small group games where the children can learn to take turns, such as *Duck Duck Goose*. (see table _____)
- Set up more difficult manipulative centers that help improve fine motor movement. You can have them sort, stack, count, or play with smaller items than before (smaller beads, small plastic chain links, etc.)
- Set up "soft areas" where the children can try a somersault down a foam wedge or on a mat. Allow children to explore what they can do and the cushion is there in case they need it.
- Play creative yet simple tag games outdoors or gymnasium. Everyone must hop like a frog, baby crawl, or gallop like a horse. A simple way to make sure everyone has a turn is to shout out a child's name and have everyone chase after that one child. Once they are caught, call out the next name of the person to chase. Make sure you let everyone have a turn.
- Encourage the children to climb on the jungle gym or swing. Make sure it is a safe height and they are closely supervised.
- Sing more songs and add various large and small movements. They would enjoy adding simple sign language to some familiar or new songs.

Category 3

- Set up a little basketball area with low hoops and encourage bouncing the ball and trying to shoot a basket. You can even use a laundry basket on the ground.
- Create picture cards of everyday objects that you use. Have one child look at a card and act out how they use the item. Let the other children guess what he is acting out. (e.g. jump rope, spoon, popsicle, etc.)
- Set up a net outside in the grass to give the children a target when they kick a ball.
- Let the children pour their own drink at snack time. Provide a small pitcher and mark the glass to prevent spills.
- Have a picnic lunch and allow the children to spread peanut butter and jelly on bread to make their own sandwich.
- Teach children to do some simple dances, such as the twist (twist your arms and waist in opposite directions) or the Charlie Brown (rock back and forth from the front foot to the back foot).
- Set out short obstacles for the children to jump over. Try to keep it at about 6 inches or shorter for this age.
- Make butter in a jar. Put heavy cream and a pinch of salt in a clean jar with a lid. Close the lid tightly and have the children shake it to make the butter. Have them take turns shaking because it takes a while. You may add yellow food coloring to make the butter yellow.
- There are many great children's CDs out there that have movement songs you can do with your children. *Kids in Motion* is a CD with songs called Animal Action, where the children are asked to move like different animals.

Child's Name: _____ Teacher: _____ Date Initiated: _____ Date Completed: _____

Activities 3 ½ - 4 Years Continued

Creating My Way — Creative Exploration

- Make a necklace out of an "o" shaped cereal or candy that is safe for them to eat.
- Have the children practice cutting on straight, curvy, and zigzag lines. As they improve, provide shapes or pictures for them to cut.
- Create collages based on your theme. If you are talking about the zoo, have them cut out all the animals you might find in a zoo. If you are talking about the color blue, have them cut out anything they can find that is blue. After they cut, then have them paste them on thick paper.
- Make bubble paintings. Make a runny solution of non-toxic paint and soap. Place some of the paint solution in a small cup. Have the child blow into a straw in the cup to make bubbles. Either place paper under the cup or place the paper on top of the bubble to make bubble paintings.
- Have the children create treasure maps. Provide pencils, paper, crayons, and any other supplies to help draw a map.
- In Circle Time discuss different colors of skin, eyes, etc. Let each child use a mirror to look in and draw a picture of what they see. Point out eyes, nose, mouth, ears, hair, glasses, etc. Extend the activity with an art activity. Encourage them use the special skin color crayons to color it in according to their own skin color. Post the pictures and share each child'

Category 4

- Make paper bag puppets according to your theme. If you are discussing the community, you may want to make a police officer puppet or doctor puppet. If you are discussing farms, you may want to make a pig or horse puppet.
- Have the children help create a colorful alphabet to decorate the room. Make a page with a giant bubble letter for the whole alphabet. Give them various materials to fill the letter in, such as buttons, small beads, paper scraps, or rice.
- Let them color on blank paper without guidelines. Just let them be as creative as they want to be.
- Give them paint mixed with glitter to paint sparkly pictures that will glisten in the sun. Have them help make a giant sun for the wall. Cut out a large sun shape and have them work together to paint it with yellow and orange glitter-filled paint.
- Make sock puppets. Give the children a plain, white sock and have them draw a face on the end of the sock with a fabric marker.
- Create smelly pictures by adding a spice, such as cinnamon, to paint.
- Cut sponges in different shapes that relate to your theme. Let the children dip these sponges into paint to make prints of the shape on paper. You can use this paper to cover a bulletin board while you work on the theme. (e.g. Cut moons and stars out for animals that are awake in the nighttime.)
- Let the children use glue to draw on cardstock. Encourage them to draw shapes or letters with glue and then have them sprinkle colored sand or glitter on the glue and then shake the extra off. For easier cleanup have them shake the extra sand or glitter onto a paper plate or tray that you can put back in the containers to be used again.
- Discuss different colors of hair and textures (curly hair vs. straight). Provide the children a yarn color that closely matches their hair color so they can glue it on pictures of faces to create a self-portrait. Label the portraits with each child's name Hang them up and use them as "teachable moments" throughout the next week.

Child's Name: _____ Teacher: _____ Date Initiated: _____ Date Completed: _____

Activities 3 ½ - 4 Years Continued

Exploring Our World — Activities to Explore Cognitive, Pre-Math, Sensory and Science

Category 5

- Dig up some worms and dirt, and then put them in a clear container for the children to observe. Be sure to return the worms to the ground at the end of the day, so you don't have to explain why the worms don't move anymore.

- Encourage and help children count how many times they can hop or jump.

- In a sand box or outdoor sand table, give the children buckets, shovels, and other toys to help them create. Try giving them a few buckets of water and explore what happens to sand when it is wet.

- Use the colorful counting bears to work on some different skills. Give directions such as, make a line of bears and put the blue bear first, take 4 bears out of the bucket, or sort the bears by color.

- Play the mirror game. Tell the children, "Do what I do." Then make different hand movements and/or facial expressions. They then mirror what you do. You can always end by placing your hands in your lap so they are calm and ready to listen.

- Play guessing games with food. Provide a variety of common foods with a distinct smell. Hide the food or have the children cover their eyes and smell the food. Have them try and guess the smell. You can use the same idea with taste, too.

- Purchase or create pair puzzles. This means there are only two pieces to the puzzle and a picture on each piece is related. You can make puzzles with opposites, shapes, or rhyming words. (e.g. One piece has a picture of an empty glass and the other piece has a picture of a full glass.)

- Make a weather bear (or other animal). Laminate the bear and different weather related clothing, and then put velcro on them so the children can dress the bear according to the weather. (e.g. If it is raining outside, then the children can put a raincoat and rain boots on the bear.) This is a great activity to do everyday.

- Give the children a chance to compare weights of different or same objects such as several different blocks that they can compare. Change the objects you use on a regular basis to provide a variety of practice. Use the seasons to guide your weight and size selections such as (several sizes of pumpkins during Fall).

- Create cards of different shaped objects and then make the silhouette of that object. Have the children match the object and its silhouette.

- Make 5-10 cut outs of each different shape. You can make them a variety of sizes and colors. Make a corresponding envelope for each shape. Have the children sort the shapes into the envelopes.

- Make a die of colors out of a small cardboard box (make sure it is a cube shape). Use a different color on each of the six sides. Have the children take turns rolling the die and telling what color they rolled.

- Set a tightly sealed ant farm out at the science table for the children to observe.

- Discuss animals and the different names for their babies. (e.g. cow – calf, dog – puppy, bear - cub, pig – piglet, etc.)

- Do a sky watch. Take your blankets out and lay on the ground during recess. Discuss what they see. Later extend the activity encourage painting, drawing or use of paper scraps to cut and glue what they observed.

Child's Name: _____ Teacher: _____ Date Initiated: _____ Date Completed: _____

PERSONAL SUPPLY INVENTORY CHECKLIST

CHILD'S NAME: _____   **DATE:** _____

SUPPLY	FULL	HALF	NEED MORE
Disposable trainers			
Plastic pants covers			
Underwear			
Shirts			
Long pants			
Short pants			
Socks			
Diapers			
Disposable wipes			
Waterproof paper for diaper barrier (such as wax paper)			
Diaper ointment			
Other:			

To find your specific
State's Licensing, Rules
and Regulations go to:

http://nrc.uchsc.edu

APPENDIX

B

Gloving

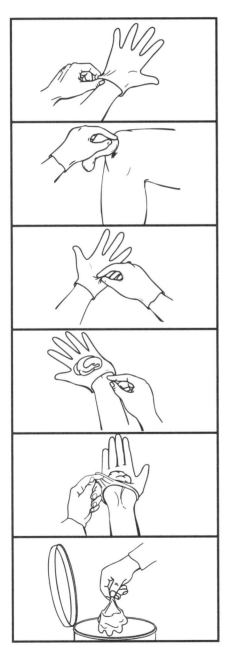

Put on a clean pair of gloves.

Provide the appropriate care.

Remove each glove carefully. Grab the first glove at the palm and strip the glove off. Touch dirty surfaces only to dirty surfaces.

Ball-up the dirty glove in the palm of the other gloved hand.

With the clean hand strip the glove off from underneath at the wrist, turning the glove inside out. Touch dirty surfaces only to dirty surfaces.

Discard the dirty gloves immediately in a step can. Wash your hands.

Reference: California Department of Education. *Keeping Kids Healthy: Preventing and Managing Communicable Disease in Child Care.* Sacramento, CA: California Department of Education, 1995.

To find your specific
State's Licensing, Rules
and Regulations go to:

http://nrc.uchsc.edu

Washing Hands

APPENDIX

C

1) Wet hands.

2) Add soap.

3) Rub hands
together.

4) Rinse
hands with
fingers down.

5) Dry your
hands with a
towel.

6) Turn off
water with
paper towel.

7) Toss the
paper towel in
the trash.

Good Job!

Reprinted with permission from the National Association of Child Care Professionals, http://www.naccp.org.